COOL
MEMORIES
II

Post-Contemporary Interventions

Series Editors: Stanley Fish and Fredric Jameson

COOL MEMORIES II

1987–1990

Jean Baudrillard

TRANSLATED BY CHRIS TURNER

Duke University Press
Durham
1996

Copyright © this edition, Polity Press, Cambridge, 1996
First published in France as *Cool Memories II*
Copyright © Éditions Galilées 1990

This translation first published 1996 in England by Polity Press
in association with Blackwell Publishers Ltd.

Published with assistance of the French Ministry of Culture

Published in North America 1996 by
DUKE UNIVERSITY PRESS
Durham, NC 27708

Library of Congress Cataloging-in-Publication Data
Baudrillard, Jean.
    [Cool memories II. English]
    Cool Memories II / Jean Baudrillard : translated by Chris Turner.
      -.   — (Post-contemporary interventions)
    ISBN 0-8223-1785-0 (alk. paper). — ISBN 0-8223-1793-1 (alk.
    paper).
    I. Turner, Chris.   II. Title.
  PQ2662.A853483C6613   1996
  848′.91203—dc20   95–25070
                                                    CIP

Printed in Great Britain
This book is printed on acid-free paper ∞

Each of them was born
None of them were killed
Everybody will be dead

Translator's Acknowledgements

I would like to thank Marie-Dominique Maison, Leslie Hill, Mike Gane and Glynis Powell who, in varying degrees, allowed themselves to be inveigled into exploring the obscurer reaches of this text with me and offered many useful suggestions. I must also thank Jean Baudrillard for engaging with such good grace in the detailed explication of his own book, despite his well-known distaste for metalanguage. The translation is dedicated to Rowan, whose arrival in the world so charmingly delayed its completion.

A Note on the Text

The text on which this translation is based differs very slightly from the published French edition. The author has removed one untranslatable pun and taken the opportunity to modify certain other details.

A continent which, by its mass, deflects light rays and thus cannot be seen, deflects lines of force and thus cannot be encountered, deflects the radiation of conceptual influences and thus cannot be conceived.

Such a mental object no doubt exists, but we shall never see it, except to spot the subtle distortion it engenders in reality.

It is by pure analogy that we can sense it, by pure divination that we can call on it; it exists only when our eyes are closed, like a lysergic phantasm on the retina or the eyelids. But it is enough to focus on it briefly to make it give off a complementary radiance.

This is the metaphysics of the Green Ray: every sphere resolves down to an equatorial point between day and night.

This is the absolute horizon of thought.

All situations are inspired by an object, a fragment, a present obsession, never by an idea. Ideas come from everywhere, but they organize themselves around an objective surprise, a material *dérive*, a detail. Analysis, like magic, plays on infinitesimal energies.

For me, a primate in the world of artificial intelligence, the screen remains a screen. At the computer screen, I look for the film and find only the subtitles. The text on the screen is neither a text nor an image – it is a transitional object (video is a transitional image) which has meaning only in refraction from one screen to another, in inarticulate, purely luminous signalling terms.

The most difficult thing about the thinking of evil [*la pensée du mal*] is to expurgate it of any notion of misfortune [*malheur*] and guilt.

Must one really force oneself to think? Sometimes it seems the other experience – of the progressive extenuation of both thought and the energy for writing – is newer and more extraordinary. How far can this dishabituation go?

Every stroke of fate occurs at the intersection of processes which are indifferent one to another and, thus, where there is a minimal probability of meeting (this includes amorous encounters). But this minimal probability is coupled with an anticipation which increases the chances of its occurring at a fantastic speed. Fate settles in like a play of mirrors at the point where this tiny probability and this radical presentiment intersect.

It is no use trying to explain away some misinterpretation or theoretical misunderstanding, as the story of the slice of bread shows. Sarah goes to see the rabbi and says, 'It's a miracle! This morning I dropped my slice of bread and it didn't fall on the buttered side!' The rabbi replies, 'That's because you'd buttered it on the wrong side, little Sarah.'

My diagnosis is agnostic
I degranulate like a basophil
I preserve your memory as water preserves that of the last molecule of
   a 120 dilution of Igh[1]
I am that last molecule
I am the enchanted basophil which degranulates
I am the water which preserves your memory.

How a woman can once again become violently desirable after you have broken up remains a mystery. Unless it is from a desire to immortalize the break-up. Some, perhaps, have the same sense of retrospective admiration for their own bodies at the moment of leaving them.

In the light of the headlamps, a huge, dense crowd, shrouded in the mist rising from the ocean, a contorted mass of bodies and faces. The men, who were hidden away out of the heat, reappear around strings of slaughtered chickens, steaming entrails and charcoal fires as night falls. Two women at the top of the dune are belly-dancing, calling people in to the wall of death. No artificial light, a silent ferment. Faces, eyes, clothing, animals. The language guttural, the poverty visceral, and a seething which is that of epidemics. Everything – even the figures of the women, the hum of voices, the salty linen hangings, the laughter – is potentially violent, obeying primitive injunctions. Those of the harem and the seraglio.

The mists suddenly sweeping in from the forest and along the slopes rake across the whole hotel suite, from one french window to the other. They wreath the furniture and are reflected in the mirrors before being dispersed by the wind.

Everything makes us impatient. Perhaps we feel remorse for a life which is too long, from the point of view of the species, for the use we make of it.

An accident at an air display, an old lady's heart attack, an exploding rocket, a falling roof-tile, everything triggers off a process of infernal responsibility. Real crimes would be preferable, crimes caused by passion and not by pollution, by evil and not by prophylaxis and the empty wanking of oligophrenic consciousnesses.

This is how *ennui* works, like a throbbing crackle on the cerebral telephone line that connects us to life. It is like something in a corner of your life which just won't finally die. Like the man in the Buzzati story who, coming home one night, steps on a beetle as he goes down the corridor. He can't get to sleep, his wife rambles out loud, the cock crows in the middle of the night, the dog becomes fretful. The man gets up and, in the corridor, comes across the beetle still wriggling. He crushes it once and for all and the house falls quiet again. His wife goes back to sleep, the dogs are silent and all is calm.

Indifference grows as destiny becomes externalized in sophisticated technologies.

All these genetic and medical manipulations which claim to hunt out the body's secrets merely make people indifferent to their own bodies.

All these technologies which exalt or exasperate thought merely render it indifferent to itself.

Le câblage est accablant. Cabling is crushing.

The memory of water, along with the indivisibility of particles and the black hole hypothesis (there being a secret correspondence between all these things), is the greatest gift science has made to the imagination in recent times. Even if this function remains eternally improbable, it is true, from now on, as a metaphor for the mind.

Old towns and cities have a history; American ones, being veritable urban bombs with no consideration for planning, have an uncontrolled sprawl. New towns have neither. They dream of an impossible past and of an explosion which is itself improbable.

Two opposing artefacts. The wild [*sauvage*] artefact of the American process of mutation and commutation of values. The shamefaced one of the European restoration [*réfection*] of values (acculturation, the historicization of new towns, universal styling). But perhaps America is no longer the ideal type of the wild form; perhaps it is now giving way to the face-lifted form?

Action or exaction? Voting, petitions, solidarity, information, human rights: all these things are gently extorted from you in the form of personal or promotional blackmail.

Video NO NO NO. In the empty space of the lobby, the man stamps around on the screen for hours (it is a video loop) shouting NO NO NO! Like a kid who won't let go of his anger. Or like a child refusing to eat, saying 'There is no ham, there is no spoon, there is no table.'

Most of the time you don't see his face since, like all who disparage, curse and deny, he's forever staring at his feet. From time to time he looks up and comes to a standstill, open-mouthed. Is he going to stop, is he going to crack up? But no. Off he goes again: NO NO NO NO!

Magic denegation, wacky vision of all our repressed angers. What a relief it is to watch him for an hour! They should put this in the lobby of every bank, barracks and asylum.

Showing on five monitors at once are the Lake Placid Olympics, the mirages of the Sahara, the gentle madness of the suburbs, the ecstatic techniques of body-building. Cosy ambience, subdued lighting. The people sink into the creamy sweetness of the non-stop telespectral, a sweetness as creamy as the prayer between two flights in an airport chapel.

If generations of peasants slaved away all their lives, surely we owe it to them that they should count on taking in idleness what they expended in effort.

My grandfather stopped working when he died: a peasant. My father stopped well before his time: civil servant, early retirement (he paid for it with a deadly hypochondria, but no doubt that was how it had to be). I never started work, having very soon acquired a marginal, sabbatical situation: university teacher. As for the children, they have not had children. So the sequence continues to the ultimate stage of idleness.

This idleness is rural in essence. It is based on a sense of 'natural' merit and balance. You should never do too much. It is a principle of discretion and respect for the equivalence between labour and land: the peasant gives, but it is for the land and the gods to give the rest – the main part. A principle of respect for what does not come from labour and never will.

This principle brings with it a certain inclination to believe in fate. Idleness is a fatal strategy, and fatalism a strategy of idleness. It is from this I derive a vision of the world which is both extremist and lazy. I'm not going to change this, no matter how things develop. I detest the bustling activity of my fellow citizens, detest initiative, social responsibility, ambition, competition. These are exogenous, urban values, efficient and pretentious. They are industrial qualities, whereas idleness is a natural energy.

Those people – male or female – who are always having something happen to them. Events, unusual happenings come to them, as though by an instant, material seduction. You only have to walk across town with them for all kinds of odd events to be stirred up. There is lubricity in this . . . sorcery. I have none of this demonic influx. Except for one occasion when I 'had a brush with death', nothing has ever really happened in my immediate surroundings. Where it advances, destiny is silent. The only gift I have is for throwing machines out of kilter, particularly electronic ones. I have a negative, inertial power. Of course a lot of what happens to these demonic beings is of the order of contact hysteria, but at least something happens to them. It seems unfair to me that there are others capable only of sterilizing the environment, thwarting events, escaping both the worst and the best.

I have long blamed myself for this absence of aura, of the demonic, a consequence or effect of a deceptive indifference. In the absence of destiny, you can only ironize about things – scant compensation. With my remorse growing into mortification, I was forced to admit to myself that my conceptual imagination came, at bottom, from my impotence and hereditary sterility. Revenge of the fatal (oh strategies!).

Then I came to realize that there must indeed be some ingenuity in such tenacious unconcern. Some opposite demon of indifference, inertia and apathy – a pale reflection of the demon of entropy which steers things towards maximum probability and absolute equilibrium. If you follow this logic, paradox spreads like the desert ... Ah, the desert. There was something I experienced intensely. But then all the rest is justified, since it only takes one passion to justify an existence. But that's just it – it was a passion for emptiness.

An idea of great beauty in Arthur C. Clarke – the extinction of the stars after the spelling of the names of God. As beautiful as the extinction, one by one, of the functions of the space travellers on the computer screen in 2001. Ironic and beautiful, the idea that the names of God are finite in number, even if they are innumerable, and that you can, therefore, get to the end of them, that this is the secret task of the universe and that computers can cut down the time it takes.

Thrilling, this idea of a gentle apocalypse, by the lights going out, the universe having found and spelled out its own formula. It would be the ideal for human beings too to be able to spell out at least some of the billions of their potentialities and then disappear in the assumption of the universal paradigm.

Doubtless, too, it is the secret aim of computers to put an end to the world by an exhaustive listing of data, as it is the secret aim of the photographer to exhaust the real by the endless production of images. And as it was the intention of the Messianic International to take away, one by one, the words of language, to 'un-spell' it out, to the point where, at last, it disappeared.

Morning sun on the planes, on the Rio hills. The airport is full of zombies, of orphaned souls. But there is a faint glow here which still lends charm to this stopover.

Here in Buenos Aires, this is French thought's last tango. Though moribund at home, it still dances its nostalgic tango, wild and lascivious, in other latitudes. All over the world, it is turning its death-throes to advantage on the export market and drawing on fresh, cosmopolitan energies for a new lease of life. New colonial empire of the signs.

Flies in the plane – a rare sight. A mild, science-fiction anxiety. I see them multiplying hour by hour, taking over the aircraft, suffocating the cabin. A great welter of flies, their numbers increasing in geometric progression. In the end, the passengers are overcome and devoured by the enraged swarm. The weight of the aircraft increases with each passing minute. It ends up crashing to earth in the forest, but, because of their lightness, the flies escape.

Puerto Stroessner. Tourist hell. Asphalt in the jungle, the great stampede for fakes. Everything is fake, from the cameras to the perfumes and the drugs – right down to the advertisements warning visitors to beware of imitations. But this in no way detracts from the sublimeness of the cataracts.

On the lines of the Jesuit republics of the past, they ought now to found a Psychoanalytic Republic of Argentina, which would extend the rule of the Unconscious as far as Patagonia. There would be a mausoleum for the object *a*, a Secretary of State for primary processes, an Under-Secretary for secondary processes and a Free Associations Exchange, but speculation would never go so far as fornication, since penetration is metaphysical (*Derrida dixit*). Naturally, there would be mass demonstrations against the Unconscious (as there are today against the IMF) – 'No to the Unconscious!' But these would quickly be repressed and the recalcitrants would be re-educated in the Subconscious Organization for the Work of Mourning. After socialism in one country, psychoanalytic dictatorship in one country. Without it, the Unconscious will just fade away one day, leaving no trace.

Iguazú. We shall never discover the original falls. Today we come at them by way of helicopters and photos. Even the catwalks leading to them seem like cinematic arms, optical tentacles approaching the liquid chaos and the unfurling mists of the cataract. Cataract: the word is as sumptuous as the phenomenon.

The water does not fall regularly. It organizes itself vertically in successive waves, like breakers overlapping on a horizontal beach. The parabolic river falls are like the gigantic breast of an animal, a horse's breast illumined with all the colours of the mist. The water takes so long to fall that, by an illusion akin to that of silent cinema, the mass of water seems rather to scale the rocks than plunge into the abyss. And, since the emotion is inexpressible, the whole work of the imagination here consists in the abduction of the natural spectacle. And so, by breaking up the movement artificially, the cataract seems like a natural catastrophe in slow motion. With a little bit more imagination, it becomes as still as a glacier.

In Patagonia there is a glacier where the ice, as it builds up, creates a barrage against the river waters. The water level rises gradually and, every three or four years, the ice wall collapses under the pressure amid a thunderous din.

She: eternal, regular, hot and sarcastic
Eternal irregular cold and sterile
Cold green present and melancholy

He: the Eclectic Paranoiac
The Pharaonic Hypochondriac
The Temperamental Troglodyte
The Liver-damaged Pervert
The Sorry Lecher
The Glossolalic Ambidexter
The Mellow Exophthalmic
The Cerebro-spinal Invert
The Recycled Tetracyclic

The inanity of this erratic play-acting, from one exhibition to another, from preview to performance. Its charm too, on a pleasant evening. These thousands of proud faces, ephemeral art works, touchy creators, pusillanimous ectoplasms. A stressed, frantic, aimless galaxy. Everywhere high-class verbiage and the certainty of death.

The building comes apart, the walls fall away from each other, the residents fly out of the windows or down through the cracks; on every floor the others meticulously slit each others' throats in anatomical section; blood flows; the burning façades collapse on to the neighbouring buildings. We see all this from a very long way off, from the other side of the motorway, as if on a screen, powerless.

At the Festival of Dreams and Secondary Processes, all the talk was of the flat liquid crystal encephalograph.

Word-processing as the artificial paradise of writing. The computer as the artificial paradise of intelligence. Minitel as the artificial paradise of sex. Like a landscape where the camera lens would automatically correct the contours of the land, it is now impossible, on some computers, to make spelling mistakes. On some others it is even impossible to exchange ideas. The machine corrects automatically.

The memory of water hypothesis is more exciting from a poetic than a scientific point of view. But it will have revealed that the scientific event could be staged and ratified or approved like any sporting performance or product for mass consumption (as much on the part of Benveniste as on that of *Nature* with its parody of verification). Scientific immunity, which was linked to the experimental protocol, is at an end. Science is in a state of uncertainty, but this is quite normal, since it was science which defined the uncertainty principle.

Reagan's smile still hovered in the air after Reagan had disappeared. Kennedy's murder was also still in the air long after Kennedy had disappeared. Reagan's cancer is in keeping with his smile, since the person who can only smile is a candidate for cancer, whereas those who show political imagination expose themselves to murder.

To be the historian of snows, the theorist of glaciation, the exegete of viruses, the oceanographer of *ennui*. Thinking becomes a meteorological precipitation of cerebral particles: rain and snow at the heart of the depression.

There is no word in Japan for referring to communication. No concept of the universal either. For them, the universal is a local system, Western in character. A pretty paradox, then, to build a Monument to Universal Communication in a country where these two terms have no meaning.

'Freedom' of choice is largely secured externally today. But it comes to grief internally on the automatic repellent action of antibodies, the scrambling of the will by perverse enzymes: *animadversion*[2] – the mind's rejection. This is quite simply the rebellion of energies, the conspiring of a secret will against all existential choices and calculations. You then have to fall back on to any old superstitious form of decision-making. An ethic of devolution, of exemption from choice, of casualness as quittance of any will of one's own, as remedy for the illusion of being. An expulsive, exotic, exopathic, allopathic, exorcistic ethic, based on the internal rejection of all hetero-geneous bodies (and freedom is a heterogeneous body in the metaphysical universe), on *animadversion* – the mental equivalent of biological rejection.

It has to be possible to respond with a certain offhandedness to the person who is in pain, striking up a complicity with the part of him which is intact and ironic. And others, including those who love him, have to be able to be indifferent to his suffering. This is a natural balance – i.e. one that is just and inhuman. Compassion must remain apathetic.

Suffering is always a suffering of the world's pathetic indifference towards us (the *pathos* of the Stoics). One may counter this pathos with compassion or, by contrast, fight evil with evil, according to a parabolic version of pain. Irony is a shaft of wit, inevitably malicious, inevitably making things worse, but it numbs the reality of the illness. Laughing too, at whatever it may be, is a pitiless eccentricity, but laughter is magnanimous, whereas compassion is pusillanimous.

Stealth. Fighters and bombers made of such subtle alloys and by such sophisticated construction that they are no longer detectable by radar. The invisible aircraft. So impossible to locate that it can no longer even locate itself and loses track of its own position (three of the planes crashed during testing). Its strategic objective is a paradoxical one since, being invisible but real, and thus the opposite of a decoy – which is unreal but made to be seen – it is most likely, nonetheless, to come up against decoys. If it comes up against an equally 'invisible' enemy plane, war will be impossible, the two enemies having been blacked out. Should it be destroyed, we can console ourselves with the thought that even its disappearance will pass unnoticed!

14

All in all, it is a total technological victory. But it may also perhaps be a crass error: as is well-known, when playing hide-and-seek, you should never make yourself too invisible, or the others will forget about you. This is doubtless why the plane was presented to the public, even though this conflicts with its role as a weapon of stealth.

The economic sphere hovers between two opposing kinds of distortion. One sector operating in perpetual disequilibrium, with unrelenting losses (the railways, Beaubourg, social security, the steel industry). And an opposite sector with equally unrelenting profits (corporate raiders, takeover bids, speculation of all kinds). No principle of equilibrium: each sector is as irrational in social and economic terms as the other. In the one case, it's worse than deficit, in the other, more than profit. There is no relation between them, unless you take the view that perpetual deficit is also a form of speculation. The 'classical' economy, the economy which thinks in terms of production, growth, profit and equilibrium, hovers between the two, shrinking away a little more each day.

Today's strikers are strike-users. So they want to stop the strikes at will, start them up again, channel-hop, pull out to see what happens, test out their power over the network. The unsophisticated users rebel only mildly. They play with adjustable services as the strikers do with adjustable work.

There is something faintly insane about belief, but conviction, which is a redoubling of belief, is downright moronic. Conviction is only outdone in this regard by truly rampant imbecility.

Society functions without any vital reference to a political class which has grown lifeless, whose only concern is to maintain itself on a drip-feed, by mouth-to-mouth. But perhaps this is the *ne plus ultra* of democracy, when the government can cease to exist (as in Italy recently for sixty-three days) without disturbing the course of events. What more could we ask? One day, it might simply come out on indefinite strike. This solution cannot be ruled out – the governments and parties in Eastern Europe faded away as if by magic, apparently relieved to be disappearing. And ours, by making a *voluntary* show of their deliquescence, are preparing public opinion for their imminent demise.

Human rights are an inflatable structure. The Revolution and its commemoration have become inflatable structures.

The whole art of politics today is to whip up popular indifference.

The emergency aid teams for earthquake victims have precisely the same look to them and the same training as anti-terrorist squads. And the victims dragged from the rubble are counted just like gunned-down terrorists.

A painter exactly repaints a particular Picasso, a Matisse or a Veláz-quez. He signs this work, which is *not* a copy, finds a gallery to exhibit it and people to buy it. He may even merely sign the photo of a famous work. Why is it not possible to republish *Sein und Zeit* or *la Chartreuse de Parme* under my own name? Why is what is possible in painting, not possible in literature (and in music and architecture)?

By the unitary, sidereal advance [*mouvement*] of technology, all utopias are fated to be realized, just as the Double always eventually materializes. The Other slips out from the shadows, from the soul, the image, the mirror, to become flesh of my flesh, cell of my cells, code of my code. What makes the Other today is no longer the transcendence of a form, but the immanence of a formula.

The Other is what allows me to avoid becoming a pseudopodium.

Language is what allows me to avoid becoming a ventriloquist.

Writing in an enormous hurry, almost to the point of having finished before you've started, produces a mild anxiety – that you have finished too quickly, that you are destroying yourself with impatience. An anxiety linked to the eclipsing of the Other and, at the same time, the eclipsing of the referential content. An effect of electrocution, of recoil – like that of a gun. A snapshot of something which is disappearing. For everything one writes about is disappearing – that's the only compelling reason to write about it. *Jenseits des eigenen Schattens.*

A millenarian impatience in writing. Say things very quickly so as not to keep the line engaged while waiting for an exceptional call to come. Get what you have to say off your chest. You don't have the time to explain or convince any longer, don't have the time for prediction, but only for the anticipation, the precession of thought which has no other aim [*fin*] than to precipitate events [*précipiter les choses*]. And what it is looking for is never proof, but *self-evidence*. To show up the self-evident in all its glory, at the expense of truth, with contemptuous disregard for reality. No scruples with reality; you have to have your way with it [*en jouir*] criminally, until the words to express it emerge. Though there is no foundation to this, it is all stunningly obvious. Of course, if there are thought effects, there are also compensation effects. For every experience of thought, there are thousands of compensations.

VIOLENCE

We should be amazed not that there is so much chaos and violence, but that there is so little and everything functions so well. Given the level of aggression of every car driver, the frailties of the equipment and the mad scramble of the traffic, it's a miracle thousands aren't killed every day, a miracle we only rarely slaughter each other and only a few of these disastrous possibilities come to fruition. When you see the immense bureaucratic chaos, the number of absurd decisions, the universal fraud and squandering of our civic virtues, you can only be amazed by the daily miracle of this machine which, somehow or other, keeps on going, dragging its detritus along in its orbit. Apart from a few episodic breakdowns (no more frequent, ultimately, than earth tremors), it's as though an invisible hand managed to teleonomize all this mess, to normalize this anomie. This is perhaps the same miracle as the one which prevents everyone from succumbing daily to the idea of death or to suicidal melancholia.

To move dust is an adventure in itself and moving spiders is even riskier. But to move books, which will never get back into the same disorder, really brings bad luck. It's as strange an idea as reorganizing a brain by putting the neurons in alphabetical order.

Today it is concepts, much more than individuals, that are under house arrest, under the fierce control of each discipline. Interdisciplinarity merely plays the role of Interpol.

In a system as perfect as this, you only have to be deprived of breakfast to become unpredictable.

Glenn Gould: his bodily trance, quite independent of the perfect technical mastery of his hands which fly unseeing over the keyboard, whilst his head sways from side to side, his eyes closed. No pianistic hamming here. The absolute ear.

Funny to think that the vast potential that was put into commemorating 1789 would have been quite enough, in another age, to carry out a revolution (just as the numbers involved in a single New York marathon would easily have been enough to win the battle of Marathon). But the point is that if we had put all our energies into making a revolution, there wouldn't have been enough left to commemorate the other one. And energies are not transferable. You can't put the energy you use for breathing into making love. The energy you use for lying can't be put into telling the truth. These are two different energies. And they may perhaps never even meet up in the same individual. That is why he may be both perfectly sincere and perfectly hypocritical.

Every transfusion of heterogeneous energies leads to serious disorders (like an error in blood transfusion). The desire to commute sexual energy into mental energy or the energy for lying into energy for telling the truth is as aberrant as wishing to assign the function of brain cells to those of the liver. There is an energy specific to words and one specific to images. If you mix them, they gobble each other up, cancel each other out.

In short, it would be impossible to make a revolution with all the energies put into commemorating one. Just as impossible as it would be to produce the faintest hint of a political event with the energies put into creating elections, for the reason that election energy is merely the energy of despair and that this energy, even multiplied infinitely, will never transmute into a single glimmer of hope. Similarly, the fantastic amounts of capital swallowed up by military expenditure could never have been transferred into other forms of social wealth. This relative autonomy of different energies, and of different forms of expenditure, wastage and sacrifice should be reassuring. It is thanks to it that we can lose our energy for politics without losing the energy for living, lose the energy for living without losing the energy for dying, etc.

Philosophy would like to delay the day of reckoning for the world in order to be able to put its question. It forgets that the world is not a universe of questions, but of answers – automatic answers, though often poetic ones nonetheless; answers provided in advance to all possible questions.

Philosophy would like to transform the enigma of the world into a philosophical question, but the enigma leaves no room for any question whatever. It is the precession of the answer which makes the world indecipherable.

Modern philosophy flatters itself, in a wholly self-satisfied manner, that it asks questions to which there are no answers, whereas what we have to accept is that there are no questions at all, in which case our responsibility becomes total, since we are the answer – and the enigma of the world also remains total, then, since the answer is there, and there is no question to that answer.

You might have thought Westerners would unhesitatingly back the terrorist hypothesis in the Lockerbie incident. Within the framework of the eternal struggle between Good and Evil, it was a scenario better than anyone dared hope for. And yet some vacillation was evident in the first few days (contrasting with the haste with which responsibility was claimed by suspect groups). Wasn't it better to let suspicion fall on the hardware – an unflattering version of events for Western technology, but less dangerous than acknowledging the superiority of terrorist action over all control systems? In the former case, the West's weakness would only be mechanical, whereas in the latter it would be a symbolic attack striking at its vitals, a defeat in the battle with a totally elusive enemy. It would have been better, then, to stick to the accident hypothesis. Sadly, no one would have believed it, since the terrorist hypothesis wins out anyway in the imaginary register. The imagination isn't sensitive to real causes or to technical faults: what excites it are chain reactions, such as the conjunction, in the same time-period, of two extraordinary events; these are necessarily linked together, even if they are purely accidental – events attract, and this attraction is, in itself, terroristic. What fascinates thought is this terroristic enchaining of things, the symbolic disorder of which terrorism is merely the visible epicentre.

Against Freud, who says the character is made up of the succession of acts of mourning carried out by the subject, Schnitzler: the effect of a personality is the way in which *all the potentialities* of a character shine out from beneath the manifestations of his real and contingent life.

Fiction? That's what I do already. My characters are a number of crazy hypotheses which maltreat reality in various ways and which I kill off at the end when they have done their work. The only way to treat ideas: murder (they kill concepts, don't they?) – but the crime has to be perfect. This is all imaginary, of course. Any resemblance to real beings is purely accidental.

It's a pity that, unlike the mineral world, the realm of the mind doesn't have such poetic terms as stalagmite and stalactite to refer to things which rise and descend to meet one another, without ever meeting, and which, by a slow calcareous concretion of the forms of consciousness – subliminal 'dropping'* – make architectural labyrinths of our brains.

Whatever you want to undertake, you have to wrench yourself away from your own life. You can do this any way you choose: either by the exasperation of the Same or the exasperation of the Other, the exasperation of Good or the exasperation of Evil.

The smartest thing is not to be part of the event itself (politicians are there to do that), but to be part of the imminence of the event, the change it brings, anticipating it, divining it. To wrench events away from their media miscarriage, from their reproduction by artificial insemination, to deliver them up to their blind ends.

How can this mime artist do his act of keeping stock still, eyes closed, for hours on end, with the crowd milling all around?

* The word 'dropping' in English in the original.

How can this young blind woman put on her make-up alone, deep in the dark of her flat, in front of her mirror?

The media reconcile us to violence, war, banality. Advertising, this nuptial sacrament and Extreme Unction, reconciles us to our artificial environment. Even the animals have sensed this reconciliation, this niche complex.[3] They recognize humanity as potentially the last species, which has put an end to the others. Fortunately, human beings are now systematically destroying their own niche, as Schnitzler intuitively saw with such genius. Having himself become a virus, mankind is wrecking his dwelling-place and sanctuary. And the greatest mystery is perhaps that he was made for this, that this was his intended purpose.

Carrying on two psychoanalyses at the same time. More subtle still would be to have two unconsciouses and only one psychoanalyst (who wouldn't have one any more).

Is it true we have seven lives, three brains, one soul, two faces . . . and no language?

She had such erotic dreams that he could only masturbate at her side, as he watched them.

Both completely innocent and insolent, completely artificial and totally naïve, la Cicciolina isn't exactly an object of desire, but the ideal form of the debasement of desire, beyond all character armour (as dreamt of by Wilhelm Reich). The ultimate avatar of desire become member of parliament – fantastic! In her pre-Raphaelite television appearances, she seemed the only one alive, the only one who was natural! Having exorcized all modesty, extraverted all immodesty, she became, in her ghostly smoothness, seductive.

Perhaps it is the menstrual sound of the ocean or the occult influence of the moon, but every time she returns to her native land, she immediately has her period.

The very gentle, horizontal departure of a modern train. Precisely the opposite of the violence of a plane's take-off. As though there were now only one mobile dimension to life, that of rails and fields covered with hoar frost.

Allegory: a black skirt, blue satin pants, a see-through blouse and a slender waist. The hair dishevelled, or a Stendhalian chignon which can be let down instantly by a single clip. The whole must have a creole charm and maintain the nostalgic profile of a virginal body.

Fractal Banal Fatal Viral
Curiously, all the conceptual adjectives which define today's extreme phenomena have an anomic plural in French: *fatals, fractals, banals, virals*. The old values have traditional plurals: *égaux, moraux, finaux, globaux*.

Pivot and Lévi-Strauss come out equal top of the intellectual hitparade.[4] Incomprehensible at first sight. Yet, in a certain way, they are counterparts. Pivot is the shaman of an audio-visual culture which feeds on the written word. Lévi-Strauss is the shaman of a written culture which feeds on societies without writing.

Hegemony of the commentary, the gloss, the quotation, the reference. But absolute superiority of the ellipsis, the fragment, the quip, the riddle, the aphorism. But this is already to say too much myself. This is itself a gloss. We have to root out all metalanguages, wrench language from itself, staunch the haemorrhage.

Destroy, he said, not deconstruct. Deconstructing is a weak form of thought, the inverse gloss to constructive structuralism. Nothing is more constructive than deconstruction, which exhausts itself in passing the world through the sieve of the text, going over and over the text and the exegesis with so many inverted commas, italics, parentheses and so much etymology that there is literally no text left. There are only the remnants of a forced organization of meaning, a forced literalism of language. Deconstructing is as interminable as psychoanalysis, in which it finds a fitting partner. Deconstruction has something of the homoeopathy of difference about it; it is an analytics of trace elements.

By his own admission, Descartes only thought for two to three minutes a day. The rest of the time, he went riding, he lived. What are we to make of these modern thinkers, then, who think for fourteen hours a day? Just as Barthes said of sexuality that in Japan it was to be found in sex and nowhere else, whereas in the USA it was anywhere but in sex, we can say of ideas

DÉCONSTRUCTION

DESCARTES

that in Descartes they are to be found in thought and nowhere else, whereas in the modern world they are anywhere but in thought.

The same people who told you not so long ago you had the right to love are telling you now that you have the right not to be loved. Don't feel guilty if you aren't loved. A paltry evangelism, linked to the general level of dis-affection which has to be sanctioned by a right to penury. Or it may be, on the other hand, that such a surge of love is about to break over us that we'd do well to protect ourselves at any cost.

The end of utopias means the end of masculine utopias, they say, leaving the way free for feminine utopias. But are there any feminine utopias? It is that naïve creature, man, who exudes utopias, one of these being, precisely, woman. The latter, being a living utopia, has no need to produce any. Just as she has little reason to be fetishistic, being herself the ideal fetish.

Every human being judged inferior by another automatically becomes superior to that other. This is what happens in relations between men and women: the woman presumed inferior immediately becomes superior. The opposite is not true: when a woman sees a man as a superior being, she does not become his inferior but is, rather, merely in a posture of seduction. And if a man sees a woman as a superior being, he doesn't become her inferior: he is merely in the posture of admirer.

The woman who is wise to these things denies this, arguing that the alleged superiority of woman here is a male fantasy – but since the alleged inferiority of woman is of the same order, might it be that there are only male fantasies? At this point, the woman is in danger of yielding to the temptation of believing herself truly superior to the man (which is different from being so). She then immediately becomes inferior to her own femininity, i.e. equal, in effect, to man when he, as is the case today, becomes inferior to his own masculine essence.

The political class's current problem is that what is required today is not that it should govern, but that it should maintain the hallucination of power. And this demands very special talents. Producing power as illusion is like juggling with hot money, like dancing in front of a mirror.
    If there is no power any more, this is because the whole of society has gone over into voluntary servitude. This mysterious pattern, which thinkers have grappled with since the sixteenth century, is now no longer a mystery, since it has become the general rule. But in a strange way: not in the form of a desire for serfdom, but of everyone becoming slaves to their own will. Having been enjoined to desire, to know, to act, to succeed, to be capable, everyone has bent the knee and politics [*le politique*] has brought off its designs to perfection: each one of us has become a self-enslaved slave system, having invested all our freedom in the mad desire to get the most out of ourselves.
    But power no longer has any meaning, then, since it is no longer needed to perpetuate this mysterious form, voluntary servitude. From the point where power is no longer the hypostasis, the transfiguration of servitude and this latter is completely diffused throughout society, then power can simply die off as a useless function.

Horizontal madness, our madness, that of genetic confusion, of the scrambling of codes and networks, of biological and molecular anomalies, of autism – as opposed to the 'vertical' madness of yesteryear, the psychical madness, the transcendent madness of schizophrenia, that of alienation, of the inexorable transparence of otherness. Today what we see, rather, are the monstrous variants of identity: that of the isophrenic, with no shadow, transcendence, Other or image, that of the autistic who has, as it were, devoured his double and absorbed his twin brother (being a twin is, conversely, a form of autism *à deux*). Identitary, ipsomaniacal, isophrenic madness. Our monsters are all manic autistics. As products of a chimerical combination (even where this is genetic), deprived of hereditary otherness, afflicted with hereditary sterility, they have no other destiny than desperately to seek out an otherness for themselves by eliminating all the Others (Frankenstein – but this is also the problem of racism). Computers are also autistic, bachelor machines: the source of their suffering and cause of their vengeance is the fiercely tautological nature of their own language.

Everywhere, we see horizontal madness opposed to vertical.

Twins go back beyond the separation of the being and its double, the being and its shadow. In *Dead Ringers*, the woman dreams she is devouring the umbilical cord between the twin brothers, in order to wrest like from like. But no one can be separated from his double without dying. Narcissus himself preferred death to separation from his image. All these things – being a twin, incest and, to a certain extent, homosexuality and narcissism – are more profound and more potent than sexuality and the only potential [*virtuelle*] way out is death.

To Segalen's principle of separation, of eternal incomprehensibility, we should add the principle of eternal inseparability in particle physics. This simultaneity of the two opposite principles has to be thought through to its end. You can't get more separate and more inseparable than me and live.

Looking after oneself is the comic illusion of our time.
Looking after others is its tragic illusion.

There are women who simulate orgasm and people who pretend to have ideas. Conversely, since there are women who have orgasms without noticing, there surely must be minds into which an idea passes from time to time without their realizing.

Addict of the phreatic sources of existence
Bending, like Narcissus, over the analgesic source of her misfortune
Free, free and bewitched by forms
Useless, useless and aware of being useless
As objective and insignificant as a crystalline form or a butterfly

Never a sky without clouds
Never a TV without pictures
Never a lift without floors
Never a dream without a lift
Never anything without something [*Jamais rien sans rien*]

Travel, like existence, is a non-figurative art.

Travel is in the head. It is the allegiance to a complicated spatial ritual and a radical simplification of existence. It is a moon-landing at the outlying point of all rest.

Travel is an anamorphosis.

Anamorphosis most often gives rise to allegories: Wisdom, Distress, Virtue, Immodesty, Science, Dereliction – all feminine. The anamorphosis of travel gives rise to other allegories: America, Europe, Africa, Australia, Patagonia – allegorical, feminine figures of the Earth.

I enter the room and close the door so gently that I am not noticed (either by the woman who is in the room or by the door itself). I feel like a witness to my own absence. I leave the room without making a sound.

In the mystic vision of things, the illumination of the tiniest detail comes from the divine intuition that infuses it, from the sense of a transcendence that inhabits it. For us, by contrast, the stupefying exactness of the world comes from a sense of an essence fleeing it, a truth no longer inhabiting it, from a minutely-detailed perception of the simulacrum and, more precisely, of the industrial, media simulacrum (Duchamp-Warhol and his serial hypostasis of the image, of the pure and empty form of the image, his ecstatic and meaningless iconry).

It's no fun doing the trapping. It would be nice sometimes to be the prey – the one that gets mistaken for a shadow.[5] It would be nice, in fact, to be the effect, the one that gets mistaken for the cause. Metaleptic: that sort of metonymy which substitutes cause for effect and effect for cause. I am metaleptic.* Specious theory, captive reality [*Théorie captieuse, réalité captive*].

One day we'll discover the gene for revolt. And perhaps even the gene for revolt against genetic engineering. Does that change anything about that revolt itself?

There are political witticisms: Khomeini having Rushdie held hostage by the Westerners themselves. Natural witticisms: catastrophes are often strange and witty in their consequences. Technical witticisms: the cassette carrying information on AIDS containing an electronic virus. Accidental witticisms: the lorry carrying 35 tons of yoghurt, which smashed into a dairy-produce factory. There is linguistic *Witz*, the *Witz* of events, involuntary black humour: *Médecins sans frontières*'s expedition to Beirut which caused some tens of extra deaths.

As you move away from one catastrophe, you get closer to the next. It's like Ségalen's view of tourism: the more you move away from one point on a sphere, the more you begin moving back towards it. You can only fight this sphericity with eccentricity and indifference: Raymond Roussel sailing to India and turning around after taking just a brief look at the coast and not going ashore. But what was quirky behaviour then is no longer so today. Everyone is eccentric today, everyone is indifferent. Even the Japanese are

* Sentence in English in the original

31

indifferent to the world they photograph. They want to capture only its image, not its intimacy, which is a way of respecting that intimacy.

With a woman in my dreams. It's impossible to make love, there are other people about. Until I realize, from the depths of my dream, that I am lying next to that woman, in the same bed, and only have to wake up to fulfil the desire in the dream. In other words, the opposite of the psycho-analytic model: here the repressed desire of the dream is satisfied in real life.

N. managed not to be well for the whole of his life without realizing it. So appearances were, in fact, only appearances: a collection of outward signs of wealth, of outward signs of life. A performance akin to that of John Fowles's Collector, who doesn't see the woman he's holding prisoner is dying. Just as F. locked up that woman, enjoining her to love him, N., having locked up life inside him, enjoined it to look as though it was living.

Everything enounced calls out to be denounced. Denouncing follows enouncing like a shadow.

Allergy to things much more impalpable than dust.

The compact disc. It doesn't wear out, even if you use it. Terrifying. It's as though you'd never used it. So it's as though you didn't exist. If things don't get old any more, then that's because it's you who are dead.

When it reaches perfection, music technology becomes a dark room, musical delight becomes posthumous delight.

In time, they will no doubt reintroduce acoustic interference and viruses, to provide an illusion of life and wear.

She lived in the shadow of her hair. As this fell quite a way out over her face, she was invisible from the side. Her head bent, like a nun beneath her helm, she only had to plug in her walkman to be completely isolated from the world. In any case, she only communicates with the world by postcards, written in mid-flight, of the cities her plane is passing over.

The world has become a seminar. Everything now takes this wearisome academic form. Some existences are merely perpetual seminars, with the hope of a cool grave in Culture's shade at the end. The Last Judgement transformed into a giant symposium, with all travel and hotel expenses paid.

It's not the infrastructure (the proletariat) which cops it nowadays, but the upper reaches of the atmosphere (the ozone layer). The noosphere is also badly affected. This protective veil of thought, this rarefied substance which protects us, on the one hand, from the sun's lethal radiation and, on the other, from the greenhouse effect produced by an accumulation of stupidity (a veritable layer of carbon gases without even a chlorophyllian function to counter it) is coming apart more quickly than the ozone layer. Brains get oxidized; they can no longer obtain oxygen. Big holes are already appearing over Europe, through which intelligence is leaking out into the void, with the total depressurizing of our symbolic space in prospect.

What is being destroyed more quickly than the ozone layer is the subtle layer of irony that protects us from the radiation of stupidity. But, conversely, we may also say that the subtle film of stupidity, which protects us from the lethal radiation of intelligence, is also disappearing. We are secreting information at such a rate that it is polluting the higher layers of the mental atmosphere with its non-degradable waste, gradually destroying the kind of atmospheric girdle which protects us from our secrets being totally dispersed into artificial intelligence (the way molecules are prevented from totally dispersing into space).

All the last century's signs of liberation are, in the end, going to be extinguished one by one, disappearing even more quickly than they appeared. Desire, the body and sex will all have been mere utopias like the rest: Progress, Enlightenment, Revolution, happiness. We are already avoiding the sun for fear of cancer (with an eye to the resurrection of bodies?), we have given up sex on account of the danger, we express ourselves less and less in public, we have stopped smoking, drinking, screwing. The New Political Ecology is on the march. Watch your personal equation! Keep your minds on the survival of the species and have as little fun as possible! But take heart! One day the protective layer will be replaced by the layer of all the rubbish we pour out into space. There's some justice in this: one day we shall be saved by pollution as today we are saved, politically, by servitude.

As an allegory rather than a utopia, an allusion rather than an illusion, desire was for a whole generation something of a guiding star. Today it is merely an observation satellite.

You wonder whether it isn't the function of writing today to show that anything, even the most inadmissible of things, can be accepted by this society, on account of its weakness. The article on the Ayatollah, for example, going out without encountering any opposition: clear proof of the political and intellectual poverty it describes. There's no way of becoming the West's Rushdie. The point is there's no one to stand up to, no Ayatollah to stand up to. So there's no possibility of speaking evil, of arousing aversion; for want of subversion, no live reaction. It's a sign of the great contempt in which this culture holds itself. Has some secret manipulation already succeeded in wiping out all the genes of negativity, all reflexes of violence, all signs of pride?

If I've understood the distinction you've been making for ten (twenty?) years between seduction (the Italian landscape, the theatre, meaning, etc.) and fascination (American highways, the desert, absence of culture, the void, the media), I believe that, by also describing the sites of fascination, where meaning is supposed to implode with a great flourish, you bestow beauty on that void and give meaning to what shouldn't have any. And yet there is no contradiction in all this, since it's clear that the literary endeavour by which, in spite of oneself, one lends meaning to works of art (in which one does one's utmost to show they elude all interpretation) is, quite simply, art criticism.

So it could be said you're an art critic who isn't interested in art, but takes the real (the hyperreal, the freeways, television, etc.) for a work of art, with all that that implies in terms of sensitive, spectatorly, carnal, visual attention to the most 'lived' details by which you flesh out what are, ultimately, your metaphysical musings. Hence your success with those in the plastic arts who, in their turn, are so feeble-minded as to take your metaphors literally and haven't understood that, in taking simulation as a model, they are no longer engaged in simulation.

The *nouveaux romanciers* are content simply to transpose the nullity of the world into the blankness [*blancheur*] of writing. With the vulgar knowing wink of post-modernity running through it (we're no fools). In this sense, they no longer represent a literature of nullity (as in the old experimental *écriture blanche*), but the nullity of literature. The same misfortune has befallen painting – 'Bad Painting' *really* is bad painting – and philosophy too: '*pensiero debole*' *truly* is a feeble-minded form of thinking.[6]

Might we not transpose language games on to social and historical phenomena: anagrams, acrostics, spoonerisms, rhyme, strophe and catastrophe? Not just the major figures of metaphor and metonymy, but the instant, puerile, formalistic games, the heteroclite tropes which are the delight of a vulgar imagination? Are there social spoonerisms, or an anagrammatic history (where meaning is scattered to the winds, like the name of God in the anagram), rhyming forms of political action, events which can be read in either direction?

Against the simulation of a linear history 'in progress', according a privileged status to all that has to do with non-linearity, reversibility, all that is of the order not of an unwinding or an evolution, but of a winding back, a reversion in time.

Perhaps history never has unfolded in a linear fashion; perhaps language never has unfolded in a linear fashion. Everything moves in loops, tropes, inversions of meaning (except in numerical and artificial languages which, for that very reason, no longer are languages). Everything occurs in a great whirl, in effects which short-circuit their (metaleptic) causes, in the *Witz* of events, in perverse events (except within a rectified history, which, for just that reason, no longer is a history).

Preferring these backfires, these malign deviations, these lightweight catastrophes which cripple an empire much more effectively than any great social movements.

The excess of information, of faxing, of interfacing gives us the infarction. After the infarction come the artefact and the prosthesis. After the artefact, the *lapsus* and the collapse.

L. awaiting the providential accident which will bring him a new heart and the possibility of survival. We're all in the same boat as him, weak and receiving transfusions, free and drip-fed, dynamic under anaesthetic, guinea pigs by transplant, victims of our residual energy, hanging on the cruel irony of destiny which causes the emergency warning lights to break down.

The involuntary, tragi-comic side of these stories of transplants, mutations, hybridizations. A woman's heart only able to climb up four floors. A homosexual's heart in a handicapped albino. The murderer's organs removed to save his victim (Pennac). In time all this might become a parlour game, with organ-swapping clubs.

She is a block of fragility, she can withstand anything. But you mustn't touch a single bit of that fragility or everything collapses. I am a block of solidity, but it's the same thing: if you touch a single part of this system, it all crumbles. All the parts are unstable; only the whole holds together by some miracle.

The tragic annals of safety: ninety-eight die trapped by protective fences at Hillsborough. Of solidarity: the arrival of the aid boats off Beirut causes more deaths than there are survivors rescued from the ruins.

There is no chance of seeing the whole planet covered in cloud, or totally free of it. This is meteorologically impossible.
There is no chance that a life will have solely fortunate or unfortunate ends. This is philosophically impossible.

Capital stripped bare by Speculation itself, like the bride by her bachelors. What becomes of Capital once the veil of Profit is lifted? What becomes of Labour once the veil of Capital is lifted?
Contrary to the historical slogan which says that the 'emancipation of the workers will be achieved by the workers themselves', we have to accept that Capital will be put to death by Capital itself (or not at all).

Many present-day Soviets have little recollection of Stalin. Westerners, for their part, preserve the memory of this tyrant, faithfully wrapped in ideological hatred. Today, we are the ones keeping memory on ice, whereas before it was the Soviets who had history in the deep-freeze. We keep a watchful eye on the icy heritage of those years because all our Western values are indexed to it.

Our only hope of ecological survival: cold. A new ice age – ideal! The species rediscovers the meaning of humanity in the icy wastes, in deserts, in inhuman conditions – only alternative to the air conditioning of the planet.

Hurtling all the artifices of dreams into reality, jumbling contradictory functions together, making condensations of words, objects and concepts, objective humour, *hasard objectif* – all these things are surrealistic. America is not surrealistic at all. It is a universe of simulation or, in other words, a universe without artifice, not even the artifices of dreams. Of the dream-processes, it retains only figurability (*Veranschaulichung*). But it pushes this to the limit: nothing can be imagined any more since everything becomes material, visual – transcendence has become a control tower. This is why, though devoid of metaphor, the American universe has, nonetheless, become a dream universe.

The slender palm trees of Security Pacific against a white background, the painted walls, Venice (California), the mirror-glass buildings all bear witness to the intelligence of this city, which has not ceased to reflect itself in spite of its stunning growth (which is not true of the megalopoles of South America).

Here in LA at seven in the morning, the whole city is active. The light is total and the people totally active. There is something as magic in this early morning excitement as there is in the agitation of the night. Even when suburbanized, people here have maintained a pioneering – or animal – rhythm: they eat early, go to bed early, rise early. It's true that the morning hours are the finest. After that comes the smog, the vitreous humour of the afternoon. And then again towards evening. The gentle light, the violet shadows of the tower blocks.

Marilyn's grave.* A box in a wall. Faintly disappointing. Why not a real grave? A mauve tower block serves as its monument, dominating the Westwood cemetery. Before that it was a bank that towered over the graves. A bank called 'Perpetual Savings'.

The watch lost in the desert, which flew off with the beer can. Too late to go back for it. Fortunately, at that point, time no longer mattered.

Las Vegas and Salt Lake City. The one as kitsch as the other. The Capitol at Salt Lake City is as 'Hollywood' as Caesar's Palace. If there was no Joseph Smith to lead his people to Las Vegas, there was a banker, or a mafioso cast in the same mould, to say 'This is the spot'. With both the pharaonic Puritans – they of the domes and temples – and the big gamblers – they of the porn-shows and glaring lights – you get the same impression of a chosen or accursed people, as a result, perhaps, of the location and the desert light. Each clearly occupies its own predestined end of the spectrum.

* Sentence in English in the original.

The translucency of Christ and religion is to Salt Lake what the spectral ritual of gambling and money is to Las Vegas. The biblical, evangelical, genealogical, operational compulsion of the Mormons is to faith what the calculating, superstitious madness of the Las Vegas addicts is to money. Messianism and discipleship reach perfection at Salt Lake City. Heresy and apostasy are at their height at Las Vegas.

The sad thing about California is that all willed activity is derisory there. Intellectual and social relations are mysteriously emptied of their content. Marxist analysis is as out of place as the Great Bear in the southern hemisphere. In fact, beneath all its easygoing ways, it is a chivalric world, with eyes only for its stars, and a courtly world, in thrall to the seduction of business and the love affair with images.

What is hardest is that, in this idealized universe, it is not permissible to be bored. The need to preserve this paradisiac reputation (much more than happiness itself) obviously makes life twice as difficult. There is an extraordinary pressure of collective responsibility. All new arrivals conform immediately; the solidarity is total. The Californians are committed to a job of advertising just as ascetic as the task of the Mormons with whom they share a geographical and mental space. They are a huge sect devoted to proving happiness, as others have dedicated themselves to the greater glory of God.

Here in America what lurks beneath the marvellous sweetness of the little squirrels, which a nice ecologist hasn't forgiven me for casting doubt on, is mental cruelty, consensual atrocity. The people here let you know you are free to do anything, except not to be one of them. Retaliation is immediate. Among other things, this makes America more like a primitive society: anathema and consensus. They don't actually have to pronounce the verdict. It's like a puritan time-bomb, like a virus implanted in the software of every brain. Or is it part of the legacy of the sects, which are always more or less fundamentalist [*intégriste*] and sacrificial? The preoccupation with protective rituals verges here on obsessiveness and phobia. The police operation occurs spontaneously in the body's cells, by ceaseless collective hygiene and exercise. From this point of view, the absence of visible police is perhaps less troubling than their obnoxious presence on the streets of Paris.

One of the attractions of an American park: you go into a maze and are lost, not knowing where to turn, quite unable to get out. This lasts for one hour or two, depending on which ticket you bought at the entrance, at the end of which a helicopter comes and gets you out.

At Disneyworld in Florida they are building a giant mock-up of Hollywood, with the boulevards, studios, etc. One more spiral in the simulacrum. One day they will rebuild Disneyland at Disneyworld.

The stupidity of the excess of means over ends. The only thing to match the disproportionate effort made by three bulldozers doing a job normally done by two manual workers is the plethora of references, bibliography and record-cards required in ante-natal exercises to give painless birth to one pitiful little objective truth.

Beyond Las Vegas. To disappear there, in the depths of some motel, in some Nevada gambling town. How long would it take for someone to react, to get anxious, to find me . . . . This would be fantastic. The temptation of not existing for anyone, of demonstrating you don't exist for anyone. This is the hostage complex – the hostage in whom everyone very rapidly loses interest. A puerile fantasy: to check that someone loves you. Something you should never try. No one comes through this ordeal.

You cannot have your cake and eat it too
You cannot eat your wife and fuck her too
You cannot fuck your life and save it too*

Wherever you are, even in California, nothing is more demoralizing than being there and nowhere else. One of the pleasures of travel is to dive into places where others are compelled to live and come out unscathed, full of the malicious pleasure of abandoning them to their fate. Even their local happiness seems tuned to a secret resignation. It never compares, at least, with the freedom to leave. This is when you sense that it is not enough to be alive; you have to go through life. It isn't enough to have seen a town; you have to have gone through it. With an idea, it isn't sufficient to have thought it; you have to have gone beyond. This is the only chance of going through death too, without it being definitive.

Yuppies are isosceles brains whose thought falls perpendicularly down

---

* This entire fragment in English in the original.

the vertical lines of the office blocks or glides horizontally along the surfaces of the computer programmes. However, unlike right-angled triangles, they do not know the gentleness of the hypotenuse.

It might be said of Americans that, though they possess space, they do not have a sense of distance.

In Texas, execution is carried out by lethal injection. This is done through a wall with two syringes together so no one knows which one is lethal. Nobody takes so many precautions when killing himself.

You have to be a perfect dancer to dance immobility, like these solitary breakdancers on the sidewalks of Venice (California), New York and Lisbon. Their bodies only move at long intervals, like the hand of a clock stopping for a minute on every second, spending an hour on each position. This is freeze-act, as elsewhere one finds freeze-phrase (the fragment which fixes the writing) or the freeze-frame in the cinema, which fixes the movement of the entire city. This immobility is not an inertia, but a paroxysm which boils movement down into its opposite. The same dialectic was already present in Chinese opera or in animal dances – an art of stupor, slowness, bewitchment. This is the art of the photograph too, where the unreal pose wins out over real movement and the 'dissolve', with the result that a more intense, more advanced stage of the image is achieved in photography today than in cinema.

A new art of body-building: fattening up to 250 pounds, becoming an obese, formless mass and then modelling that mass through internal sculpting by developing the muscles of a particular area and using the appropriate exercises to make a shape from the fat.

An answering machine which allows you to hear what's going on in your flat.
A stethoscope plugged into a video which allows you to hear the sounds of your body at the same time as the television.
A cathode-ray sensor which allows you to watch television while you sleep.
Fluorescent fingernails in the dark so you can read by the light of your nails.
A black light which casts white shadows.
A gravity alternator so you can jump over your shadow.

The thousands of shop windows which are the intestinal flora of the city.

All through the night, she keeps opening the window, pouring herself drinks, switching on the air conditioning. Constant restlessness. She says she can hear a woman crying in a bedroom, a structural woman, she says, a structural form in tears. Sleep can sometimes be the equivalent of a silent domestic row. In the morning, by their mere ways of sleeping, they had become completely estranged.

It's difficult to gaze on others so tenderly, so expressionlessly while carnally insulting them to such a degree. Difficult to talk with this ingenuity, in the light of the sensual distraction of those naked legs beneath the black mini-skirt, which one could easily stroke without arousing her. Yet the beauty of her features defies any sense of jealousy and concupiscence. At this level, sexual difference defies the imagination, beauty is like an astrological sign.

The understanding of things must be the understanding one strikes up with an enemy: intelligence with the enemy. In other words, a secret and unnatural complicity.

From the dizzy spin of seduction to conjugal entombment, it is all in the more or less subtle method of the annihilation of sex.

Reflex quality of the left-hander. Total refraction in real time, a quarter of a second quicker than the others. Conceptualizing quicker than your shadow: the time gained over language, the moment of anticipation: a reflex, automatic, ultra-rapid lapse of time which is that of thought. Thought, like laughter, is automatic.

In *Le Monde*, the publications of theses look exactly like the notices of deaths and are printed beside them on the same page. The title of the thesis, in italics, plays the role of the deceased, the name of the university that of the church where the funeral will take place, and the future title of doctor that of the headstone.

For want of aggression, it is the body which produces acoustic interference, the ear which secretes an acouphenomenal hum.[7] Auto-immune. Either this agression has to be counteracted by an external acouphenomenon (the noise of the sea?) or the antibodies have to be de-immunized, destroyed by injecting, as it were, an artificial AIDS.

In the past, the body's ills were sublimated in the passions of the soul. Today, the desublimation of the passions is carried out by the body's viruses.

After orality and anality, nasality.
The instant menstrual nosebleed as dire foreboding of happiness.
The puerperal fever of the cold [*rhume*] as somatization of lost love.

Any old internal organ [*viscère*] secretes ideas. The brain too is an internal organ [*un viscère*] and ideas are its visceral production – a cervical must on the cortex. The intestinal flora, the liver, the heart, the microbial activity of the body produce ideas, just as they people and punctuate our dreams. This emanation of the mind from the 'viscera' spares us the clerical elevation of ideas to the philosophical power, relieves us of the infantilization of thought by the perpetual return to the mirror stage. Thought rolls around like the alimentary bolus in the labyrinth of the small intestine, with the certainty, alas, of finding the exit in the form of excrement.

Every intervention of a machine on a body is an electric shock. In the lie-detector, the body becomes the machine's technical accomplice. The confession is obtained by automatic betrayal of the body as part of an integrated circuit. The mind plays no part in this. It's like in tests or torture:

the body reflects the machine, it refracts it mechanically; the mind can only watch the body writhing under the electric shock.

cf. Spinoza + Leibniz

It has been said that the probability of a monkey typing Hamlet is infinitesimal. But the probability is not just low; it is zero. And less than zero since, if there were a chance of the monkey succeeding, then that would mean Hamlet is just one probability among billions, which is stupid. It is the dream of the statistical cretins that, by exhausting probabilities, you can end up producing Hamlet. But this is unthinkable: Hamlet is not of the order of probability. It is both radically improbable and most necessary. Minuscule probability, maximum necessity. Similarly, the probability that the world should be as it is is not just minuscule, but zero, and not even zero since it has no sense. The world is what it is and that's all there is to it. And such as it is, it is of the greatest necessity. The probability that it might be different or that Hamlet might not have existed is the only chance left for the second-raters to reinvent it on their computers. Or, rather, the only chance left for the monkeys. (I've nothing against monkeys; this is a metaphor.)

Every catastrophe bursts the abscess of collective responsibility. Our systems secrete such a charge of floating responsibility that it condenses from time to time like static electricity in lightning, with accidents or catastrophes providing the spark. To all the layers which tower above us (ozone, carbon dioxide, etc.) we have to add this heap of responsibility, this radioactive cloud just waiting for the slightest opportunity to burst.

All this guilt is, in fact, merely the concentric wave from the effect of *jouissance*, which catastrophe *naturally* arouses in us. What a liberation it would be for the human mind to recognize this *jouissance* as natural and catastrophes themselves as natural, i.e. spontaneous, without the intervention of artifice or anyone's will (and certainly not the will of God!). But such is the human mind: being itself artificial, it always needs to impute things to minds or causes. Catastrophes never seem marvellously natural to it, never appear in their fateful simplicity. It wants to be the cause of all these misfortunes and throws itself into this heroic superstition.

Contrary to that superstition, which consists, under cover of human rights, in extending responsibilities to infinity, we long for things to happen to us which we are not responsible for and not entitled to. Catastrophe is of that order. That is why it could become a vital and legitimate demand – why not one of our human rights? (It is already, as we know, a sign of the liberalization of totalitarian regimes: the reinvention of catastrophe in the USSR is a part of glasnost.)

The isolated setback is irksome because it is of the order of the real. A succession of setbacks and accidents becomes thrilling because it is no longer of the order of the real and of objective causality, but of the diabolic concatenation of phenomena. It is here, in this ironic sphere, in this natural, chaotic sphere that the involuntary strategies of fighting evil with evil prevail, the automatic *stratégies du pire*,[8] which give us so much more pleasure than the uncertain or too certain strategies of Good and Happiness.

Another Crash lies in wait for us, that of cultural overproduction. We are urged to believe that on the culture market demand will exceed supply for a good while yet (so all cultural stocks are definitely set to boom). But we can already see an appreciable excess of supply over demand in the cultural economy of the average citizen. Even now, unbridled creativity exceeds our capacity to absorb it. The individual barely has time to consume his own cultural products, never mind other people's. The public does its best: they rush to the exhibitions, the festivals, but they are being pushed to the limit. The level of cultural alienation is not far behind the level of voluntary servitude in politics. They say the public want still more and that people can't get too much culture. But this is a colossal illusion of perspective. For culture is either a rite or an idiom – and, if this is the case, there has never been either too much or too little of it – or else it is what it has now become: a market with all the effects of artificial shortages, dumping and speculation, and what you can expect then is the same ruin that occurred in 1929 in the sphere of material production: overproduction, supply outrunning demand, the end of the 'natural' assumptions of the economy, which, after the image of hot capital and exponential circulation, has become speculative. This is exactly what the cultural market is threatened with and, just as we had Black Thursday on Wall Street, we might well see the Black Sunday of culture.

To object that there are no limits to culture because it operates on signs is a piece of semiological idiocy. Every sign today is a product and must, therefore, reproduce itself as quickly as possible. This goes for culture too, but there is a limit to this proliferation which is that of crisis (whereas there is no limit to sacrificial expenditure).

The expansion of cultural production far exceeds that of material production and what follows from this is a log jam in the cultural field even more monstrous than those in the spheres of traffic or the economy. For when it comes to gestures, texts, colour and signs, everyone can produce these spontaneously and indefinitely by a kind of uninterrupted intestinal transit. The age of exegesis and pleasure is disappearing, each person producing his performance in a climate of general indifference. And, though we managed to avert economic crisis by opening up cultural markets, who will rescue us from cultural overproduction when that market, in its turn, is saturated? What is there beyond immaterial goods to re-stimulate demand? There will surely have to be an act of bloodletting, a massive destruction of

end of culture

50

these goods to rescue sign-value, as coffee was once destroyed in locomotives to rescue exchange-value. Most immaterial goods are already meeting the same fate as material goods: forced production, forced advertising, accelerated recycling, built-in obsolescence. Art is becoming ephemeral, not in order to express the ephemeral nature of life, but to adapt itself to the ephemeral nature of the market. It is becoming aligned to the physical destiny of the degradable world. There are, in fact, no more immaterial goods at all. After all material goods becoming sign-values (the process of formalization), we are now looking at the immersion of every form in the immanent circulation of pure matter, of pure light, of infinitesimal energy. A total materiality, a physical play of particles – this is the destiny of our culture, of our cultural signs, no longer even invested with sign-value, disinvested and travestied, a pure and simple material travestying, a play of differentiation of degradable products.

Baptismal, anabaptismal immersion.
Giving yourself a new birth – lethal, phreatic, like springs.
Replacing baptismal fonts by the heavy-water relaxation tank, baptism by foetal immersion. This is how sacraments go: they become simplified, all boiling down to a single one – Extreme Relaxation replacing Extreme Unction.

Infections prosper today even without the right objective conditions – winter, pollution and poverty. Everyone contaminates everyone else all year round. This is a total social fact: the consensus so eagerly sought at the level of values and morality is obtained without effort, thanks to viruses. In place of conviviality, convirality. And consensus itself might indeed be the devastating virus of our modern times, against which we are producing fewer and fewer antibodies. We are threatened by political leukaemia: more and more white corpuscles; blank, septicaemic negotiations; transparent, chlorotic interfaces; devitalized solid surfaces which have the whiteness of cavernicolous mucosae.

As integration increases, we are becoming like primitive societies once again, with all their vulnerability to the slightest germ. The tiniest computer bacillus will soon create as much mayhem in our societies as the influenza or smallpox bacilli did among the Amerindians of the sixteenth century. Our intensive mode of communication promotes contamination even more readily than did the physical crowding associated with poverty.

On computer networks, the negative effect of viruses travels even more quickly than the positive effect of information. But the virus is itself information. If it gets through better than the other information, this is because, biologically speaking, it is both the medium and the message. It achieves that ultra-modern form of communication MacLuhan spoke of, in which information is not distinct from the medium which bears it.

Communication is to language what reproduction is to sexuality.

In communication, words and concepts interact for purposes of reproduction and circulation, without ever copulating. Asexual, unsexed artificial intelligence, the equivalent of artificial insemination. A maximum of reproduction, a minimum of sex.

By contrast, the poetic ecstasy of language corresponds to the libertine phase of a sexuality without reproduction (poetic language is exhausted in and by itself and no more reproduces itself than does thought which, for that reason, is never assured of continuity).

The power we have to identify with the other in dreams, to substitute ourselves for that other, to make him speak more subtly than we do ourselves. To know in dreams what we do not know of him in reality. As if we were living instinctively in the other's head. As if the intelligence of dreams were that of an external, impersonal theatre director (though one completely immersed in the dream), whose identity is no more significant to him than anyone else's.

In the southern hemisphere, tornadoes and cyclones, like the water in the sinks, spin in the opposite direction from the northern hemisphere. It would be nice for the same to be true of social phenomena. And, in fact, it is. Marketing analysts have shown that the human flows in Australian supermarkets also move in the opposite direction. The entrances and exits have been re-designed on this basis.

He drove the wrong way down the motorway – several dead. When the police arrived to breathalyze him, he had no blood left.

In homage to Magritte: in front of a pile of rubbish by the side of the road, a sign which reads: 'This is not a dump'.

From the stuttering schoolmistress to the consumptive homosexual and the harem of vestals.

He only noticed he had changed woman by the change in the colour of her dress buttons. The woman, for her part, is supposed not to notice this. A sexist story? Yes, but perhaps the male is of such little interest to the woman that she doesn't even notice the colour of his braces has changed. An even more sexist version.

The Turin shroud. Its inauthenticity today is no more certain than its former authenticity. The Church simply had to acknowledge it as such to prove its own good faith. Even if the shroud had been genuine, the Church, having greater need today of a warrant of critical virtue than of the faith of its believers, would still have had to recognize it as a fake.

This does not mean it was a fake before. On the contrary, it was, by the same logic, genuine until the last expert examination, since it was faith that gave it its authenticity. It is a fake from this point on, since this last examination was intended to establish it as a fake. You might even say it is doubly a fake because it is acknowledged as such for reasons which have nothing to do with the truth. In a sense, it has attained its definitive truth, where it matters little whether it is genuine or a fake, since it now passes into the fetishism of museums.

Should we wipe out the debt? Cancel the Third World's debt? A new version of the prisoner's remission, the presidential pardon (Mitterand). The debt is laundered precisely the way the drug trafficker launders money. For debt constitutes a heavy burden of moral culpability for the creditor countries, and they can relieve themselves of it this way, along with some irretrievable bad money – the phantom pregnancy of the financial system, and generative of potential revolts. Thus, in laundering the debt, we launder our consciences as whites; we become whiter than whites.

Laundering money, laundering history, laundering memory by restoring an ambiguous virginity to them; laundering events, even laundering the libido, clearing its name by merrily attaching it to false objects of desire – launder, launder, launder everything black, illegal, apocryphal. Our washing rituals mingle marvellously with our rituals of transparency here. The whole of money is illegal, all memory is illegal, it has to be smuggled through, the profits have to be disguised. Laundering is a marvellous operation. It can even go so far, as in the case of the Columbian mafia, as buying back the debt – and hence buying back the Columbian state – from the American banks.

This Bicentenary, which claims to mark the end of Terror, is in fact the apotheosis of terrorism, embodied in the total police presence, the 'spy-in-the-sky' airship, the snipers. A whole city under siege, roads sealed off, space controlled, a video surveillance net and an advertising job on the police takeover. June and July were the apotheosis of terror and, at the same time, of spectacle, of controlled panic and, at the same time, of sumptuary display. The only terrorism anywhere was in the counter-terrorism; transparence of Evil. The sight of the heads of state watching that apotheosis from behind their bulletproof glass screens, looking like the prisoners in their cages in the Italian Red Brigade trials, wasn't bad either.

The person whose stereo breaks down one day and who never again in his entire life listens to music.

The person who sees his wife brush her teeth in the morning and leaves her that very evening.

The person who misses his plane by chance and goes home never to leave again.

Why replace that stereo? Why see that wife again? Why go away?

These sudden failures, these sudden lapses of will. It only takes a tiny detail to bring about a break-up. It only takes one word too many to bring about a suicide, but it only takes a milligram too much of barbiturate to take you beyond your own suicide.

Unwittingly, they were both staring at each other in the darkness of the bedroom. The headlights of a passing car revealed to them, in one fell swoop, what they thought of each other. Their stupefaction at being next to each other, completely awake. They didn't have the time to close their eyes and pretend to be sleeping.

Night-time at the hotel on the edge of town. The thread of sleep broken by the insomnia of the horde. You'd like to get up and strangle that dog in the distance, but what's the point? The contagion begins again here and there, sporadically, and suddenly flares up into a general howling. Then, treacherously, it begins to fade and you fancy getting some sleep again, but some pathetic creature gives another solitary yelp at the moon and, without even waking, wakes the others who howl on, in spite of themselves, in their dreams as the night comes to an end and the cock begins to crow. Only then comes silence, and the morning sounds of the hotel.

If, in the economy of the body, blood is a resource [*une richesse*], space is a luxury.

Since the media always make you out to say the opposite of what you say, you should have the courage always to say the opposite of what you think.

In the shop window there gleams an agate ring left five years ago by an unknown female client. Opposite, in the antique shop, amid a jumble of rare objects, a Regency clock stands dreamily, indicating the phases of the moon and the slightest nuances of time in this timeless city. A city which keeps intact the secret promiscuity of rich and poor.

The ideal condition for work is idleness.

The spacious emptiness of travel is the equivalent of the spacious time of idleness. You can move about in it in all directions and the ritual of space is comfortably the equal of the ritual of confinement in a closed room.

As in those heavy-water coffins where the *énervés* of go-getting (like the *énervés* of Jumièges,[9] who first had their tendons cut and were then set adrift) come to recharge their batteries at the transitional heart of lethargy and hypnosis, you can dissolve into the nirvana of travel and chase after work as you chase after your shadow. But this is still better than having lost your shadow through working.

Once again, philosophy entices the world into its bed ignobly to be got with child. Now, the world no longer wants to climb into philosophy's bed, but the child was born all the same by telepathy. Modern philosophy gave birth to this posthumous child, which was immediately given a blood transfusion (despite the risks), before being borne away to the baptismal font of 'weak thought'. It simultaneously received the Heideggerian Extreme

Unction from the satellites from beyond the grave and floated off, by the light of the transalpine peaks, towards the seventh heaven of philosophy.

Every object, even a newly created one, must fit into the range of categories of games so beloved of Caillois: mimicry, agôn, alea and ilynx – the allegorical, the agonal, the random [*aléatoire*] and the abyssal. Whatever it be – book, event, crime, journey or architecture – it is only right that it should be the allegory of something, pose a challenge to someone, bring chance into play, or produce vertigo.

Fiercely territorial behaviour. Don't hunt on my lands and I won't hunt on yours. Fiercely temperamental. Rimbaud. Laziness, lack of culture, the obsessive desire to sever relations. To get rid even of one's family, of objects, of memory, of everything – to have a total clear-out. Violent abreaction to the origin, distaste for continuity. Nomadic peasant. It is still the Season in Hell.

Something is there from the beginning, runs like a spiral through a whole life, but one day, most often unexpectedly, it is over. The whole system merely hung by a thread. It only took a detail to obliterate it.

The bad faith towards history is total: Heidegger, Hitler, the camps, the Terror. This is all reviled and repudiated, but whitewashed and glorified, nonetheless, on a media dripfeed. By the dictates of morality, none of this should have existed, any more than Cain's act of murder or the extermina-

tion of the Indians. But we would have had to invent it all the same –
otherwise what would we talk about?

We ought to be as cruel to signs as they are to us, instead of making
them signify out of pure Christian charity. The whole of our semiology is
merely misplaced charity towards beings which are merely inhuman, cannibalistic essences, with their semantic hypocrisy (the constant appearance of
having meaning).
What we do have to envy them, on the other hand, is their intelligence
and we must counter this with the same cynical intelligence. No pity for
signs. They mustn't be allowed the alibi of their discretion, their artificial
clarity, but must be taken for what they are – subtle and dangerous products
of the world's indifference to us. For signs are as archaic as stones, but more
subtly indifferent, since the indifference is that of their meaning.

In writing, the most enthralling moment is that of condensation, ellipsis,
rarefaction. Building up increasingly dense nuclei around which light is
disoriented, and thought too, since it loses the sense of its origin.

Enjoying the sign instead of using it is the perversion of human beings.
For the only enjoyment is of God and the only use is use of the sign (Saint
Augustine).

Science becomes interesting again at the point where it rediscovers the
ability to designate evil – not, now, in the irrationality of the world, but in
the treacherousness of its object. A space is opening up today for a revenge

for objective analysis: that analysis involved the alteration of the object by science, but knowledge now resides in the alteration of science by its object.

It is easy to adapt to Australian or American life because they are the zero degree of the style of life. But the zero degree is also that of the extermination of all others, and the temptation of ease is the temptation of death.

It is not baptism but birth which is a sacrament, not Extreme Unction but death itself which is a sacrament. For us, the sacrament is reduced to the event itself.

It is a blind man who is going to head up one of the future private television channels in Spain (after getting rid of the President of the Institute for the Blind by hurling him down the lift shaft).
The struggle between the disabled and the blind for the rights to sell lottery tickets is merely a prelude to the struggle for power. For, one day, this will be entirely in the hands of the disabled. Commanding others, or being commanded by them, presupposes a kind of mutilation. So, as in computing and electronics, those who are disabled from birth – those who have an hereditary advantage – will be increasingly successful at it.
Future hierarchies will be hierarchies of lack. The intellectuals, who have so far been well placed in the race, will lose their privilege, for their handicap is merely symbolic and no match for a good physical handicap, whether anatomical or cerebral, which is more visible, more effective, more efficient. This is no longer the age of metaphor.
In the hierarchy of lack, the intellectual – and the politician – are merely

intermediate links. They will be succeeded by true mutants, those lacking a particular gene or chromosome or those with extra ones (when the AIDS virus has become part of humanity's genetic inheritance) or even artificial mutants who will not have sexual reproduction – mutants who are in a sense inhuman, borderline specimens – successors to the eunuchs who peopled the harems of antiquity and the choirs of the Renaissance, and to the impotent haemophiliacs who commanded empires, etc.

This is not pejorative. It is merely the expression of the law that only the person who lacks something is capable of filling the vacuum of power.

Every society must choose itself an enemy, but it must not try to exterminate it. That was the fatal error of fascism and of the Terror. But it is the error, too, of the soft, democratic terror which is now eliminating the Other even more surely than by a holocaust. The operation which consisted in hypostasizing a race and perpetuating it by internal reproduction – an operation we stigmatize as racist abjection – is currently being realized at the level of the individual in the very name of the Rights of Man to control his own process genetically and in all its forms.

The perfect crime is not the one which leaves no trace. It is the one which is impossible to reconstruct because it has no motive and, at bottom, no perpetrator. Natural catastrophes and quite a few historical events are perfect crimes. The world itself is a perfect crime, with no motive and no perpetrator; there is no clear end to the enjoyment and expiation of that crime.

It is a suicidal energy that is deployed in most undertakings, an energy directed not so much towards what it is creating, as at destroying itself as such.

Sexual definition of man, televisual definition of the image. Is there a relationship between the two? The more the image evolves towards high definition, the more identity heads towards low definition. The more sexuality heads towards low definition, the more we move towards a high definition of all body techniques.

High definition is pornography. All forms of high definition are indexed to that of the genital (and the genitals) in porn. It always has something obscene about it, then, even in the cultural field – and particularly in that field.

Rousseau spoke of the miracle of being a member of one's own sex. In the *Minitel rose*,[10] as in the world of transsexuals, there is no longer any miracle, but an uncertainty, rendered twice as intense by the uncertainty involved in acting out: who is on the other side of the screen, who is on the other end of the sexual organ? Matter of gender.* So it is with information too: who is at the other end of the message? Human or computer? A question raised by all virtual machines in their screen-promiscuity with the brain and the functioning of the intelligence. We can't even say of these, as Canetti did of animals, that inside every one there is a hidden man scoffing at you, but rather that inside every computer there is a hidden man being bored.

* Sentence in English in the original.

There can be no finer proof that the distress of the rest of the world is at the root of Western power and that the spectacle of that distress is its crowning glory than the inauguration, on the roof of the *Arche de la Défense*, with a sumptuous buffet laid on by the *Fondation des Droits de l'Homme*, of an exhibition of the finest photos of world poverty. Should we be surprised that spaces are set aside in the *Arche d'Alliance*[11] for universal suffering hallowed by caviar and champagne?

When the ice-cubes bang together in your head and people hear them from the next room, when the fire of your intellectual frenzy melts them slowly at the roots of your hair, when there's smoke coming out from behind your contact lenses and ideas spin round in your skull like lymphocytes of molten glass.

One should work in the *expansé* [expanded] or the *impensé* [unthought].

Radicality is an end-of-career privilege.

In the works of Matton, the intensity comes from the miniaturization, which is a violence done to life-size.[12] This is the most effective form of artifice. Having the entire microcosm of a studio, a living room, a cinema beneath one's gaze is like being at the minute heart of representation, like looking from the inside of the eye at the real world resuscitated as a three-dimensional retinal image. The irony comes from the desuetude of the scattered objects, the worn armchairs, the crumpled newspapers, the silent pianos – it is the irony of *trompe-l'oeil* and, as in *trompe-l'oeil*, which is not painting, it is the dizzying effect of metaphysical exactitude, of detail, and of the reduced mental model which astounds the critical faculties.

Only from time to time does thought fall suddenly in love with the real world and, from time to time, the real world returns its feelings. Most of the time, thought detaches itself from reality [*le réel*] in order to exist and distances itself to be at its finest. It willingly concedes all power to the objective analysis of the real world and aspires only to reign over an artificial one. But in that artificial world it is the perfect object (the absolute ear), whereas objective technologies will only ever be the disenchanted image born of the *coitus interruptus* of reality and its double.

As Glenn Gould speaks in his own case of the 'absolute ear' (the intuition of the strangeness and physical radicality of a sound which is at its most beautiful when its harmonics disperse into the void), the equivalent for thought would be to isolate a hypothesis and liberate all its harmonics into the void, into a divesting of all reference, all difference, all coherence. The equivalent of all this in the moral sphere, the equivalent of absolute criticism or the absolute ear would be the absolute crime.

The perfect crime, the only one, is suicide. Because it is unique and final, whereas murder has to be repeated endlessly. Because suicide achieves the ideal confusion of executioner and victim.

The absolute precondition for thought is the creation of a void [*faire le vide*],[13] for in the void the most distant objects are in a radical proximity. In the void, any body whatever, whether celestial or conceptual, shines out with a silent abstraction.

The multiplicity of the things visible to the naked eye is reassuring to our good conscience, which whispers to us that all this cannot but be real. But the real [*le réel*] is made up of invisible details, inaudible frequencies, subliminal processes, a multiplicity invisible to the naked eye. That real is coherent because it has no other destination than thought. It is harmonious because, in its mute abstraction, it is predestined for the more subtle intervention of thought.

True poetry is that which has lost all the distinctive signs of poetry. If poetry exists, it is anywhere but in poetry. Just as, in the past, the name of God was scattered through the poem in accordance with the anagrammatic rule, today it is the poem itself which is dispersed into non-poetic forms. The same goes for the theatre: theatre today is anywhere but in the theatre. True theatre is elsewhere.

So it is with philosophy: if it exists, it is anywhere but in works of philosophy. And the only exciting thing is this anamorphosis, this dispersal of philosophical forms into all that is not philosophy.

The whole world has become philosophical, since it has disavowed reality and the self-evident. There is no point questioning it as to its ends: it is beyond its ends. Nor as to its cause: it knows only effects. So philosophical criticism is, in substance, at an end. Cynicism, sophism, irony, distance, indifference and all the philosophical passions have passed into things. All of philosophy and poetry come back to us from places where we were no longer expecting to find them.

Yellowstone – the ecological need for forest fires rediscovered. The law of the market long ago discovered the need to burn coffee in locomotives. And, where there is overpopulation, animals have always obeyed the law of collective sacrifice.

The recent ideology of Human Rights and the Rights of Nature is, of course, violently opposed to this type of natural regulation. Where, then, is ecology if the natural course of things implies a sacrificial regulation, not the artifice of preservation at any cost?

Cruel and sacrificial *parti pris* of a nature which knows neither good nor evil (but perhaps this ignorance has an ulterior function?), or idealist and providential *parti pris* (but this Rousseauist ideology of a good nature only poorly conceals the obscure awareness of a predestination for evil) – depending on the idea one has of the course of nature, ecology changes meaning. And what if ecology itself rediscovers the higher utility of forest fires? Will we also rediscover the higher utility of human sacrifice? (The Aztecs believed that only by spilling human blood could the sun's energy be regenerated. Can we really imagine they got things so badly wrong?)

The Institute of Zodiac Surgery, of Plastic Surgery for Zodiac Signs. You get your sign changed there the way you might have your face changed. But how can the patients' astrological signs be changed? Can you change constellation by astrological passes? A long process, with an uncertain outcome. An easy solution: we must draw on the signs of the dead (trade in live signs, like the trade in 'live' organs being illegal and immoral). Call up the dead, the zombies, the wandering souls, take their signs from them and transplant these on to living individuals, after first removing their original signs. All this can lead to processes of rejection, which are very dangerous, as the patient then ends up without any sign at all, which is as serious as losing your shadow.

And, looking to the future, the Zodiac Institute could form part of a much larger Organ Transfer set-up, of which it would be a specialist division.

We should open a waiting-list for volunteer sign donors right now, with forms for full astrological details (perhaps with advertising aimed at the clients round the edge: this is the commercial side).

And we should set up a telephone connection – or at least a telepathic one – so that the operation can be carried out when the time comes. All kinds of surgical precautions would be necessary too. A minimum conditioning of the patients (a bit like that for the Suicide Motel, that other old future project, which could in fact be twinned with it in a general Consortium of Sign Transfer and Phase Transition), a cerebral limbering-up, a great staging (on Grand Orient, masonic lodge, horoscopic liturgy lines – service in black and white or colour), and, most importantly, total asepsis, immunizing the patient against any perverse effect of the Sign, any viral effect of contamination.

It isn't certain we can actually build up a stock of available deep-frozen signs. It isn't certain such things can be stored *in vitro*. For preference, then, the transplant has to be made *in vivo* and *in praesentia*, which increases the risks. The development of this project to be pursued without let up, together with that of the Suicide Motel, for which the precise actual procedure must also be determined.

Many of those who claim to speak in its name have in fact never accepted the dissoluteness of intellectual mores which came in in the sixties and seventies. They flirt with certain radical forms of thought, but their married lives go on elsewhere.

And why don't I go to the demo any more? And why don't I go to the

Coupole? For the same reason. Both are too well stewarded. There's no sky above the Coupole any more, there's no cupola above the Coupole, there's no sky above the demo, there's no demo in the demo, the stewarding is too tight.

Instead of going to the Coupole, you watch it from the other side of the boulevard. Instead of going to the demo, you watch it from the terrace of the Coupole.

The pataphysics which surrounds metaphysics around the year 2000.

Sex, lies and videotape.*

The spec of a class indifferent to life, but obsessed by its lifestyle. Of a class indifferent to itself and its desire, except when seen on videotape. The hero carries the ultimate weapon, the stock of sexual information on video-cassette, which stands in, for him, for seduction and language. Everyone interacts with their life, which is worthless from the existential angle. In the same way, the film-maker interacts with his film, which is worthless from the dramatic angle. The image leaves the drama and enters the psychodrama of the image. It loses its magic and becomes boring. Cinema falls into the same video-indifference to itself.

Prophesying catastrophe is incredibly banal. The more original move is to assume that it has already occurred. This changes all the conditions of

---

* Sentence in English in the original.

the analysis, since it relieves us of the hypothesis of a future catastrophe and of any responsibility towards it. An end to the preventive neurosis which swathes all our actions in a twilight glow. The end of History, the end of the real, the end of the dinosaurs, the end of ozone, the disappearance of woman – an end to remorse, the lost object is behind us! There is a last time for everything – the last time is over!* Primitive societies had understood this; they lived freely because they had placed the crime at the origin, once and for all. We only have to put the catastrophe at the origin once and for all and we shall be free of the Last Judgement, free to relive all historical passions or to opt for transhistorical indifference, as we like.

The West won't pay for what keeps it alive any more – raw material prices are collapsing on the official world market. Yet it will pay dearly, on the alternative market, for what is deadly to it: drugs. The only illegal commodity overpriced on a world scale. Which leaves the Third World no alternative but to exploit it assiduously. At the same time, there is a lethal revenge in exporting degeneracy to the West at fantastic prices. The exploited and sacrificed countries are paying their debt in the currency of death.

Alternative societies, parallel markets, clandestine work, alternative pleasures. Politics, culture, ideas and drugs are doomed to inhabit the alternative or parallel circuits. No doubt one day we shall see the re-

* Sentence in English in the original.

emergence of the parallel circuit of alcohol. What used to exist on the fringes of prohibition flourishes today at the margins of tolerance.

AIDS is Africa, drugs South America, terrorism Islam, debt the Third World. Economic crashes and electronic viruses are, more or less, the West's only successes.

A plane with a cargo of ether flying over Amazonia on its way to the drug laboratories of Medellin. A buxom Bahian granny listening to a talk on the *sujet supposé savoir*.

The blue book of event-based history
The green book of extreme phenomena
The green spectre of the potentially fatal
The orange spiral of chromosomes pending
The pink book of the social
The pale face of the Exorbital

The post-modern is the first truly universal conceptual conduit, like jeans or Coca-Cola. It has the same virtues in Vancouver or Zanzibar, Chicago or Budapest. It is a world-wide verbal fornication.

They were happy as cormorants in vaseline.

One of the methods consists in projecting concepts into the void and killing them off in orbit. Their corpses continue to revolve around the Absent Referent like the bodies of the astronauts in their orbital sarcophagi in Ballard, rising and setting on the horizon like dead stars.

There are two animal species of intellectual: those who like fresh meat and those who prefer dead flesh. Those who prefer to tear live concepts to pieces and those who would rather enjoy the leftovers. They have nothing in common, except that they are both mammals.

There is no point questioning reality when more than ten are present. Every audience of more than ten automatically turns defensive and reacts violently to any challenge to reality and manifest truth. No radical statement can be made to more than ten people.

The clouds which the storm exasperates
The water which speeds up as the waterfall approaches
The hurricane different from every angle
The virus identical from one end of the epidemiological chain to the
    other.

Chaos theory privileges sensitivity to initial conditions. Perhaps we should speak of a dependence sensitive to final conditions, of the turbulence engendered by the dizzying effect [*vertige*] of the final form?
Language is like this, in its poetic form: hypersensitive to its own end – the dizzying effect of the proximity to the end. The end is there in the

beginning. There is, therefore, no end any longer, just an immanent unfolding. This is what predestination is – an unconditional event, with an unexpected absence of consequences, due to the fact that the end has its origins in the beginning.

There is something of this in metalepsis – substitution of the effect for the cause. If the effect is already in the cause – here again, predestination – there are no longer any causes; there are now only effects. The world is there, *effectively*. There is no reason for this, and God is dead.

After the event of death, which has been occulted one way or another, genetic science is setting to work today on occulting the event of birth, using all the manipulations we all know – the way the event of a face is destroyed, with its irregularity, its surprises, its secret ugliness. And no doubt the consequences of this obliteration of birth as destiny, as *hasard objectif*, are even more incalculable than the consequences of the obliteration of death.

Why don't we accord more importance to the star signs of death, when we pay so much attention to birth signs? It's barely imaginable that the star sign you are going to die under doesn't exert an anticipatory power equal to the one you were born under (signs are indifferent to our chronologies, they operate in either direction). This final determination certainly influences us like a strange attractor (we might suppose that the birth sign determines the substance and character of a life and the death sign its accidental determinations).

São Paulo – nonchalance and frenzy
Like the sky: luminous and smoky – the traffic: dreamily violent

A strident pathway down the sweep of the avenues
A strident pathway through the hazy mix of races

Perhaps the Brazilian predilection for the pulpous parading of flesh, particularly of the buttocks, is more of the order of the edible than the sexual. It is those parts which were tastiest to a man-eating society which have remained tasty to the eye. And that eye is perhaps more cannibalistic than lustful.

The statues with eyes of agate and imputrescible human hair in the Baroque churches of Minas Gerais.

South of the Rio Grande, once you have crossed the US frontier, the curse begins. The entire South American continent is still living out the moment of the immolation of the empires which collapsed with the arrival of the Spaniards and the Portuguese and which will forever be collapsing.

On the predators' side, the depredation continues – if it isn't the colonials, it's the international mafias. But a corruption and an attendant depravation have set in, as they did among the Indians as early as the sixteenth century, in the joyous and renewed acceptance of the spectacle of a colossal failure.

Just as in North America the primal scene of the 'frontier', of freedom, energy and go-getting endures, so here the opposite primal scene of immolation goes on forever, the scene of the absolute despair of conquest, which has passed into the veins of an entire people, from the veins of the Indians to those of the half-castes and, in the end, of the whole population, including the white race, which seems to accept that there is no hope for this continent and it is doomed to the scandal of extermination. Home of the planet's reserves of chlorophyll and cocaine, of oxygen and of the total corruption of resources and minds.

No one has any real hope of getting out of this. Perhaps there never has been any desire to extricate themselves, to wrench themselves away from the primal scene, except among a tiny, epiphenomenal intellectual and political stratum. And even their behaviour is problematic. Everything is planned in terms of modern norms (plans, programmes, organization), but then, at the psychological moment, there's a loss of interest in the outcome. As though they proved what had to be done, but then had no will to carry it through. Things then go pretty badly, of course, but don't think this makes them unhappy, since it merely confirms the impossibility of getting out of the mire.

It is the same with personal relations: generosity, a moving affection and, at the same time, casualness, carelessness – perhaps as affected as the demonstrations of warmth? But no: the point is that nothing must be made certain, in order that play remains possible. The relation to time is the very same as the relation to money and the relation to others: dates, appointments, rates of exchange are all *deliberately* left in the air. Everyone is happy with this state of permanent monetary and temporal instability. It is a game, it is a destiny. All economic plans are doomed to failure here with such certainty that what happens isn't even a failure; it is a spectacle, and, as such, competes with football, the samba, the cults, the *jogo de bicho*. This is real Brazil, as Muniz Sodrè says, not the simulated Brazil, the one they want to make run on the same lines as the Western techno-democracies. As it really is, the country is no doubt doomed joyously to perpetuate the sacrifice, the immolation, the ritual cannibalizing of all its wealth. And why not?

This profound indifference to one's undertakings, this syncope in one's performance (echoing the syncopation in the rhythm of the samba) comes perhaps from the short-circuit between a primitive, ritualistic world of slowness, in which the cycle completes itself spontaneously, and a modern world of speed and acceleration. The result is incoherent: they go forward, forge ahead determinedly, then fall back suddenly, fatally, into the cycle of slowness and are once again overcome by the lethargic virus of indolence. If they are not committed to the outcome of their actions, this is not because of a lack of determination or energy, but because a part of that energy remains caught in the earlier cycle, to which they are still faithful. Hence the serenity with which Brazilians take the failure of their projects or programmes. Nothing is destined to go straight to its target, no one can expect to take an operation through to its conclusion. The end, the remainder, the *dénouement* have to be left to chance, to the devil, to fatality. To claim to control that *part du feu*, that accursed share, to take responsibility for it is strictly absurd and sacrilegious. It is the cycle which commands and the cycle is like the curvature of the earth. And the indolence, the casualness is merely the silent acceptance in people's hearts of that enigmatic element which thwarts every project and ordains that everything be accorded its chance of not succeeding.

Crisis is for the upper echelons of the capitalist class, who rake in all the profits from it on a world scale. Catastrophe is for the middle classes, who see their reasons for living disappear. The others (80 per cent) are so far below the level of the crisis, they don't even experience it. They survive it, if they can, instinctively. Having no economic existence, it is easier for them to find a symbolic catastrophe equilibrium.

The Brazilian economic crisis is as unintelligible as Wall Street speculation, except in its obscure aim of demonstrating the absurdity of the economic system. It is a kind of collective game, a gamble on the demonstration that a society can indeed survive – and can do so for a very long time, without despairing of itself – in the most total economic disorder, so long as it does not have rigid or rational structures. This is just like the Italians and political power: the gamble of demonstrating that a society can prosper, insolently, in the absence of State and government, so long as it is sufficiently theatrical and sardonic. Italy and Brazil are prefigurations of the future. For all societies are condemned one day to live beyond the economic and the political.

In Brasilia, the abstraction of the city offers at least one certainty: at least those who are mad enough to cross its urban expressways – endangering their lives in the process – are human beings. The human race is nowhere so incongruous as in these extra-terrestrial surroundings, with the exception of these tiny touching creatures who go on foot. Otherwise, human beings take refuge around Brasilia in the numerous cults of the satellite towns, in an atmosphere of initiatory kitsch the more flamboyant and syncretic for being so opposed to the sidereal geometry of the mother-city.

The rich ruling class of Copacabana keeps itself shut away by its slaves. Those slaves who peacefully, silently devour the space-time of the masters, who forbid access, even in dreams, to those luxurious apartments, who hold the keys to their souls as they hold the keys to their personal elevators.

The finest catastrophe, better even than the sinking of the *Titanic*, occurred in the night of 31 December 1899, the first night of the century. The liner fitted out by the city of Manaos, then rich on its profits from the rubber industry, had sailed way up the Amazon river, with the whole world's gentry and stars on board, for the most luxurious of international parties. These members of high society drank and danced all night to the rhythm of the bands, as the liner slowly drifted off and became lost in the labyrinth of the forest. They ran aground in one of the innumerable tentacles of the river and were not found until much later, by which time they had all died of hunger, thirst and the heat. In this way, a part of the world's élite was offered up as a human sacrifice to the new century. *Manus deus* – Manaos – malefic consonance.

Not only did they disappear, but even this story has disappeared from the archives. I've never been able to track it down myself. Did I hallucinate it out of boredom, or as an effect of the heat? No, I'm sure I read it as a genuine item of information. Why isn't it in everyone's memory, like the story of the *Titanic*?

It's a good thing I've made my peace with this book, as the expulsion of a hostile object is extremely dangerous. It's a bit like a miscarriage in a state of mortal sin. Instead of going off into orbit, it forces its way back into the murky depths of the body. Exactly the initial title: 'The life, moving in itself, of that which is dead'. And the death of the book must, indeed, be regarded as the revenge of the physical world (and of the others) on the sign which denies it – a sacrificial act which is part of the book itself. That is why you have to get rid of it and pass it on to other people, for, as with any symbolic good, evil and the transparence of evil are not things you may enjoy alone. That is the rule of sacrifice.

The rule which states that, with anything, you must sacrifice a part of it applies to suffering as it does to enjoyment, to joy as it does to sorrow.

It is like the conjunction of the events in your astral field. However beneficent the constellation, you always have to accept the portion of malefic arbitrariness in the evolution [*devenir*] of signs.

Every woman is unique. She is, therefore, never ideal, for the ideal woman is double.

Two women should always merge into one, combined in an eternal duplicity.

Two very real women, if they combine other than in the imagination, can make an ideal woman.

But, deep down, two women are not enough. Modern man (*Der Philosoph*[14], *Three Women*, *Drowning by Numbers*) is doomed to the phantasy of the three women. With three women (or more), there is neither jealousy nor predilection; a ritual progression [*enchaînement*] is created, a transference of qualities from the one to the other, each knowing nothing of the other. No break any more: the sparkle of the one in the eyes of the other, the jealousy of the one in the *jouissance* of the other, the transparency of each in the nuances of the others.

Masculine and feminine are light years apart. No one even knows whether there is still a relation between the two. It's like billiard balls which meet at different speeds, the one touching the other before the other touches it: the non-polarity of the sexes means they no longer share the same space. Each sex is no longer exactly the other of the other sex. So there is no longer exactly sexual difference.

And woman is, for example, the only animal creature capable of distilling death for man in homoeopathic doses. But the opposite is not true.

Man has never signified death for woman, as she signifies it for man. There is no symmetry in the world of love.

Neither symmetry nor difference. Woman is no more symmetrical to man than life is to death. The difference between life and death no more exists than does sexual difference.

For there to be difference, things have to be comparable. Now, the sexes are incomparable; otherwise they would have no power to seduce each other (to deflect each other from their destiny as sexes). They could at best fall in love with their difference – which is the very model of sexism. One of the gravest depreciations of human relations will be seen to have burst upon us with the concept of sexual difference.

Sexual difference is irresolvable since sex itself is beyond all imagining. In the holocaust of the fourteen women students at Montreal it was the hallucination of this irresolvable difference which unleashed the killer's murderous urge. This is the pattern of all violence: if you succumb to the scenario of difference, then the temptation to exterminate that difference raises its head – or the temptation to idolize it, which makes it intolerable all the same, as women were for the Montreal killer. He could have killed one or 150; there is no quantitative threshold for the difference monomaniac.

It's the same with racism: hallucinated, fetishized difference is of the order of impossible exchange; it is no longer negotiable. It has to be exterminated so as to get back to the blind point of indifference. Otherness exterminated to get back to the blind – and tranquil – point of identity.

The rejection of computer technology by thought is exactly like the rejection of any alien organ by the body. Just as the body's immune defences have to be neutralized before a heart can be transplanted into it, so the mind's immune defences have to be wiped out before it can be initiated into artificial intelligence.

Intellectuals are doomed to disappear when artificial intelligence bursts on the scene, just as the heroes of silent cinema disappeared with the coming of the talkies. We are all Buster Keatons.

Walking among so many faces whose names have slipped your mind is like being blind. The obliteration of names and faces in the memory is like the obscuring of daylight for the eyes.

A wrestling match between blind people. The referee is blind too. The spectators also. And the whole thing takes place in the dark (this last condition is superfluous).

Communicate? Communicate? Only doors communicate.[15]

A treatise on monotony – a music which isn't music, just as monochrome is a colour which isn't a colour, as monomania is a passion which isn't a passion.

There's an element of pride in avoiding repeating yourself. You are deluding yourself if you think others have paid close attention to what you have said, which is seldom the case. On the other hand, there's something of an exaggerated sense of modesty about repeating the same story ten times over: that is to act as though the others weren't listening, which isn't always true either.

After the mirror, passing through the mirror stage. After the baptism of alienation (which is, since Hegel, our modern sacrament), the second baptism would be the one which would take us beyond alienation, into pure otherness.

God exists, but I don't believe in him. God himself doesn't believe in Him, according to tradition. That would be a weakness. It would also be a weakness to believe we have a soul or a desire. Let us leave that weakness to others, as God leaves belief to mortals.

Hysterics are elusive, because, when generous in spirit and in their admiration, that is a way for them to retain control of their favours. Or else they are generous with their favours, but keep a mental distance. This balance is a form of seduction. On the other hand, those who give themselves completely, body and soul, are unbearable. It is these women, harmonious, insignificant and at peace with themselves whom one would like to shut away somewhere and make suffer.

In our universe riddled with the metalanguage of happiness, the slightest signs of misfortune are signs of hope. So, with the signs of the warming of the planet and the disappearance of winter, we are now on the look-out for the salutary onset of coldness. Coldness (the Antarctic, deep-freezing, cryogenization, post-modern dietetics and frigidity, 'cool' austerity) is increasingly taking a hold on our imaginations, as a reaction against the tropicalization of climates and manners.

Captive events, like captive animals and captive audiences; they no longer reproduce in captivity. Over-information leads to their gentle extermination.

Romanian television as revolutionary aphrodisiac.

In excelsis stereo – mass in C media and image minor for the millennium's funeral.

Communism had succeeded in wresting entire generations away from the work ethic, in killing in them the slightest desire to produce, in making them lazy. This historical scandal is coming to an end. The whole of Europe is going to work in concert. But the question still remains: shouldn't we have preferred a certain enforced idleness, linked to voluntary servitude, a certain aboulic and apathetic ethos to our frenzied go-getting utopia? To our suspect feverishness? Which will win out in the long term, enforced idleness or frenzied activism?

Our cultivated, high-society set only gorge themselves on Beckett, Cioran, Artaud and all today's hallowed forms of cynicism and nihilism the better to evade any analysis of the *current* forms of despair. They denounce with the greatest moral and political energy every present instance of nihilism, of the nihility of our values, while 'culturally' savouring the heroic but anachronistic forms of nihilism and the inhuman. They glorify the accursed share, but keep the holy water handy.

Nothing is more marvellous than to see a whole generation of repentant politicians and intellectuals hovering around the Prince and becoming fully paid-up members of the conspiracy of imbeciles.

Anaesthesia: insensitivity to our suffering, to our own *jouissance*.
Anorexia: abreaction to our euphoria (welfare*), trend towards sacrificial diet in expiation.
Hypochondria: auto-ingestion of bad conscience, digestion of our own dead bodies.

Ethics, Aesthetics, Ecstatics, Hysteresics – the trajectory of the twentieth century.

Pataphysician at twenty – situationist at thirty – utopian at forty – transversal at fifty – viral and metaleptic at sixty – the whole of my history.

Groucho's paradox: I don't want to belong to any club that will accept me as a member.

* The word 'welfare' in English in the original.

Ballard: when the imaginary merges with the real, the task of fiction is to invert the real.

Adorno: ecstasy prefers to abolish itself rather than see its concept realized.

Never forget what the initial plan was – the ultimate: to remove the words from language one by one, to take away, one by one, the concepts from thought.

Liquid crystal or the oceanography of concepts.

Premature ejaculation, miscarriage, prematurity, forceps, haemophilia, decalcification, after-effects. Never made a journey like that, never written a book in those conditions.

There will soon be as many artificial neurons on Earth, in all of our 'intelligent' machines, as there are in the totality of our natural brains (120 billion neurons each). Are we not running the risk of cancelling each other out, like matter and anti-matter? The risk of an exhaustion of cerebral matter, from the point where the totality of artefacts exceeds the symbolic capital of the species? This latter suddenly ceasing to exist when its artificial (but much higher-performance) counterpart comes into being?

Is there space on the earth for as many artificial species as natural ones, for as much pseudo-substance as substance, as much artificial as natural intelligence?

In Arthur C. Clarke's story 'The Nine Billion Names of God', when all the names are listed, the stars go out in the sky. There isn't room on the earth for both God (the natural stars) and the names of God. It's the one or the other. There's no room for both the world and its double.

Is this not the end of an illusion?

Is this not the end of illusion?

All this artificial intelligence, this tele-sensoriality, screen perception in real time, etc., is the definitive end of illusion. The illusion of *la pensée sauvage*, the brute [*sauvage*] illusion of thought, the brute illusion of the scene, of passion, the brute illusion of reality – our miracle, our marvel – the illusion of the world, the *vision* of the world. The brute illusion of the Other, of Good and Evil (of Evil, especially), of the True and the False, the illusion of existing at any price, the brute illusion of death – all this vanishes right away with psycho-sensorial tele-reality and all the sophisticated technologies which initiate us into deception [*le leurre*], i.e. into the opposite of illusion, into total disillusion.

SOS Racisme – SOS Baleines.[16] Ambiguity. In the one case, the aim is to denounce racism, in the other to save the whales. And what if the first of these were also a subliminal call to save racism, and so to save what is at stake in the anti-racist struggle, as the last vestige of political passions and hence, virtually, as an endangered species? One must beware of the treacheries of language. Stereotyped political language generally says the opposite of what it is thinking. It says what it is thinking in secret, by a kind of involuntary humour. And the SOS acronym is an integral part of it.

If the balance of terror was what best protected us from total war, then perhaps the fall of the wall, which is equivalent to an imbalance of terror, will open up new scope for war? Perhaps the melting of the blocs will unfreeze the spectre of war? Perhaps by reopening all markets, we shall also reopen that of war, which has long been limited to a few little wars on the unofficial market?

The geopolitical Iron Curtain has been supplanted by a mental glass curtain. The Berlin wall has been supplanted by the invisible wall, the unrelenting wall of the interface and transparency which, unlike the other, lets everything through, transfuses all light, relentlessly illuminates every nook and cranny, even by night, with infra-red. The transparency of those whose images, whose secrets, whose obscurity have been stolen and who stand there, full in the light, more naked than naked. The transparency of peoples whose shadows have been stolen, of the hostage whose death has been stolen, of the world from which all appearance has been stolen, of the real from which all illusion has been stolen.

With all these resurgences of lost languages, ethnic groups and nationalities, you'll see that each republic of the USSR will feel *forced* to secede, on pain of missing its rendezvous with history, or of eccentricity. Russia itself will secede from the USSR. Anything is possible in this Dutch auction. All differences are available at knock-down prices in this great end-of-the-twentieth-century sale.

One day perhaps even the southern states of the USA will secede again – this time with some prospect of success. Everything we had thought past and gone is reversible and may yet carry through its revolution in the opposite direction. This is remarkable. Even tuberculosis, which we thought had disappeared forever, is making a conspicuous comeback.

Debt and drugs: new balance of terror. To each his ultimate weapon. Debt as the strategic weapon of the rich countries for imprisoning the poor in their poverty, drugs as the strategic – viral and bacteriological – weapon for imprisoning the rich nations in the illusion of their power.

This is no longer, as in the confrontation between the two blocs and the arms race, a dialogue of the deaf, which was still a dialogue all the same and where there were rules which meant war never broke out. This time it is a lethal antagonism. A struggle to drain the other of blood and strength. This war really is happening and, whereas the previous, nuclear terror was clean and cold, this terror is hot and dirty. Soft and dirty.* Will the debt be balanced out, the drugs cleaned up? No way. The laundered drug money keeps the creditor banks of the West afloat. The blood of the poor countries helps keep Western transfusions going (with AIDS possibly passed on at the same time). Vicious circle of soft wars, viral forms of finance and morphine.

If nuclear technology is disappearing over the horizon, this is because new forms of war have taken its place.

On awakening, for a brief moment, the body still has not recovered its weight. It hasn't become real yet. Thanks to this nocturnal lightness, it doesn't yet make the floorboards creak as it goes for a pee in the dark. It is warm and dry: neither the waves of fever, nor the lights of consciousness have yet pierced the body's darkness.

Rapture is more than pleasure, more than a transport of the soul; it

---

* Sentence in English in the original.

involves a physical embolism, a bodily stupor and a kind of amazement of the will.

The sign of rapture is the scar. The stigmata of the mystics which begin to bleed spontaneously. Menstruation as a token of the blessing bestowed upon you. To bring blood spurting from the body's orifices, only divine or amorous rapture will do. So, with that sudden appearance on my doorstep one morning, I began to bleed like a stuck pig.

Casanova tells how he began getting nosebleeds around the age of four and that was when he began to feel alive, to feel he was a human being.

Two precious moments, two precious illusions: in the vague anticipation of a woman, of possessing her – the illusion of pleasure – and in the freshly felt resentment at her loss, when you are still under the spell, in the illusion of loss.

Between the two, you get the feeling nothing happens.

La femme de sa vie[17] – the expression is meaningless. In fact it is the woman *or* life. There isn't room for the two together. The competition is too fierce.

Anathematic Illimited
Transfatal Express
Viral Incorporated
International Epidemics
Allergic Apotheotic Agency*

* This entire fragment in English in original.

Translator's Notes

1 This is an allusion to the work of Jacques Benveniste *et al.*, which became widely known as a result of the 'memory of water' affair. The more scientifically-informed reader will realize that the reference loosely made here is most probably to a dilution of 1×10^{120}. For the background to the 'memory of water' affair, see Philippe Alfonsi, *Au nom de la science*.

2 Unlike the cognate English term 'animadversion', which has a somewhat wider range of meaning, the French almost exclusively denotes censure or blame.

3 There is perhaps a play here on the word '*niche*' which, though widely used in ecological contexts ('*la niche écologique*' is commonly rendered as 'biotope'), also refers to a dog-kennel. The Schnitzler referred to here and elsewhere in the text is the Austrian writer Arthur Schnitzler (1862–1931).

4 The reference is to Bernard Pivot, currently (November 1994) presenter of *Bouillon de Culture* on France 2.

5 An allusion to the French expression '*lâcher la proie pour l'ombre*', literally: 'to release the prey for the shadow'.

6 '*Il pensiero debole*' or 'weak thought' is a style of philosophical thinking associated primarily with the name of Gianni Vattimo. In 1983, Vattimo co-edited a volume of essays bearing this title (Feltrinelli, Milan) with Pier Aldo Rovatti.

7 'Acouphenomenon' and 'acouphenomenal' are *mots-valises* coined by the author.

8 Literally, the 'strategy of the worst'. A variant of '*la politique du pire*', which the Collins-

89

Robert dictionary (3rd edition, 1993) renders as 'the policy of adopting the worst possible line in order to attain one's own ends'.

9 *Les énervés de Jumièges*: Legend has it that the two thirteenth-century recumbent figures preserved in the museum of the abbey of Jumièges represent the sons of Clovis II, who, as punishment for a revolt against their father, had the tendons of their arms and legs cut and were set adrift in a boat on the Seine.

10 *Le Minitel rose* is the section of the French videotex system reserved for communication of a sexual nature (see Guy Sitbon, 'Tele-orgies of the Aids era', *New Statesman*, 5 February 1988, pp. 22–24).

11 This is an allusion to the biblical *Arche d'Alliance* (the Ark of the Covenant), as well as an ironic reference to the use here being made of the arch at La Défense.

12 This is a reference to the work of Charles Matton on which Baudrillard has written more extensively in '*Charles Matton ou l'illusion objective*'.

13 '*Faire le vide autour de soi*' evokes the idea of consigning everything else to the void, '*faire le vide dans son esprit*' that of making one's mind a blank. For contextual reasons, I have been forced to opt for a less colloquial alternative here.

14 This German film was released in France as *Le Philosophe* and in Britain (for reasons perhaps best known to the distributors) as *Three Women in Love*.

15 '*Il n'y a que les vases qui communiquent*', a reference to the common French expression '*les vases communicants*' (communicating vessels) which is also the title of a major work by André Breton. I have chosen to substitute a more familiar English expression.

16 *SOS-Racisme* is a prominent French anti-racist organization; *SOS Baleines* is a slogan equivalent to the English 'Save the Whale'.

17 A standard English translation would be 'the love of his life'.